SCREENING SHAKESPEARE

Understanding the Plays through Film

Second Edition

Toby Widdicombe and Michael Greer

Cover Image:
Claire Danes and Leonardo DiCaprio in *William Shakespeare's Romeo + Juliet* (1996)
dir. Baz Luhrmann
20th Century Fox / The Kobal Collection / Merrick Morton

Greer and Widdicombe, *Screening Shakespeare: Understanding the Plays through Film*
           second edition

ISBN: 0-205-63950-X

CONTENTS

PREFACE

Screening Shakespeare may be used with any edition of Shakespeare's works. It is written primarily for college audiences, and particularly for students taking Shakespeare in a major-author course or studying his works in depth for the first time.

Screening Shakespeare argues that using film helps students to see themselves as interpreters by providing a foundation for working with the complex language and historical contexts of the plays. It is written straightforwardly, and its practical approach gives students analytical tools for understanding film, but it does not overwhelm them with terminology or with theory. By treating films as cultural artefacts, it encourages students to go beyond questions of plot and form to consider seriously the historical impact of Shakespeare on our culture as well as the impact of our culture on Shakespeare.

In what follows, we've organized the discussion of the plays by genre (as is customary), beginning with the comedies and continuing through the histories and tragedies to finish with a chapter on cinematic transformations of Shakespeare's plays. Within each genre, the plays are treated in the order they were written (as far as that can be known). This approach allows readers to see how Shakespeare developed certain themes, sources, and storylines over time. The discussions of specific films in *Screening Shakespeare* are meant to be suggestive rather than definitive. Their intent is to offer insightful analyses and to pose useful questions about the films that readers may develop further in their own writing or in classroom discussions. The book also includes an Additional Resources section, which features four bibliographies, a selected filmography, and projects for writing and research. The books concludes with a glossary of film terms used in *Screening Shakespeare* and a references section.

Many of the existing books on Shakespeare films offer extensive reviews and critical commentary on the merits of particular films. *Screening Shakespeare* usually does not offer such evaluations, for they tend to draw attention away from Shakespeare to the world of the film in isolation. For readers who are relatively new to Shakespeare's plays, *almost* any film can be helpful and interesting, for each sheds light on the plot, themes, and dialogue of the plays. Each stimulates the imagination and helps anyone to get beyond the difficulties of the words on the page. The films may be used creatively to ask fruitful, probing questions about the plays and their concerns. An inquisitive approach to the films will lead readers back to the plays with new insight, with renewed energy, and with greater understanding.

HOW TO USE THIS BOOK

Screening Shakespeare is designed to help students to use film as a means to understand and appreciate Shakespeare's plays more fully. Whether you are struggling to understand Shakespeare's language or are simply looking for further insight into a particular play you already know well, watching a film version of a play can be helpful in learning more about his works. This guide will give you some critical insights and analytical tools in conjunction with your experience of the films. So, you will become a more informed, confident, and accomplished interpreter of the plays.

Screening Shakespeare may be used for independent study, or for in-class discussion as some instructors will assign films and spend time discussing, viewing, and responding to them in class. The questions in this guide may be used in large- or small-group discussions. They may provide ideas for group or individual presentations if you are expected to report to your class about a particular film. The questions were also written to serve as potential writing prompts or as topics for formal or informal writing projects.

Students may also use this book for individual study. Even if your instructor does not plan to spend class time on film versions of Shakespeare's plays, you may well find it helpful to watch some of them in preparation for class discussion. The films are *not* a substitute for carefully reading the texts of the plays since filmmakers nearly always cut and re-arrange a play's scenes in order to make them work better on screen. Indeed, speeches, scenes, and even characters may be edited out of a film version of a Shakespeare play, so it is crucial not to rely exclusively on films if you want to be successful in your Shakespeare course.

Many Shakespeare instructors and scholars do agree, however, that watching a film *in conjunction with* reading the text can be a very productive way to come to an understanding of a play. It is for this reason that scholarly introductions to Shakespeare's plays often comment on film versions (particularly recent ones) of the play being analyzed. Most Shakespeare teachers tend to be avid fans of theater and film, and they recognize the value of both for their students.

Chapter 1 provides a framework and some basic concepts for analyzing film. It explains the sort of questions and the type or critical analysis that have proved useful in viewing films based on Shakespeare's plays. It is probably a good idea, then, to read through Chapter 1 before moving on to chapters. Beyond that, it's possible to pick and choose among discussions of specific films in any order that you find useful. *Screening Shakespeare* has been logically arranged by genre (Comedies, Histories, Tragedies, and something we call "Transformations"), but it does not have to be read from beginning to end. It's designed to be help students of Shakespeare's plays who want quickly to locate background on and questions about a specific film.

Here's a strategy you could use for watching a film and reading the text as part of a multimedia approach to one of the plays. Start by reading a scholarly introduction to the play. Such an introduction will almost always cover the form of the play and its literary and historical sources. It will also give you some ideas of what to watch for as the play develops. Then read through the play once in order to get a sense of the dramatic action without getting bogged down in the details. Skip over sections of dialogue that don't at first make sense to you. Review the play by looking at the cast list (or *Dramatis Personae*) at its beginning, and see if you remember something about each of the main characters and what each says or does that matters to the plot or themes or ideas in the play.

Now you should be ready to watch the film and respond to it as an informed and critical viewer. Watch the film straight through on a first viewing. You may want to jot down brief notes about anything that you notice that strikes you as especially interesting or unusual about the film. Whatever stands out as interesting or creative (or even confusing) might provide a productive starting point for a discussion of or an essay about a film. Write your thoughts down so you can remember them the next day in class and later.

If you have time, it can be especially useful to go back and review specific scenes to reinforce them in your memory. Our visual memories do not last very long, so make detailed notes about how a scene looks when you have the film in front of you. Read the lines in the text, then watch the scene on-screen, and so forth. DVD is an especially efficient format for jumping from scene to scene, using the scene or chapter menu-function.

Once you have worked through the film a second time and written more detailed notes about it, you'll probably find that the words virtually jump off the page when you go back to reread the text of the play. On a first reading, you may find it hard to connect the words in the text to the dramatic action and events taking place on the stage. Once you've watched the play on film, though, you'll find that you remember character's accents, the rhythm and emotion they used to emphasize certain words, phrases, and lines, and so forth. You'll be able to visualize what is happening in a certain scene. You'll discover that a text that seemed static and difficult, perhaps even impenetrable, has suddenly opened up and become meaningful for you.

For each play covered in this guide, we've provided some background, discussion questions, and specific analysis. Compare these sections with your own notes and responses to the film(s). Maybe you notice things that aren't discussed in this book, or maybe something discussed here will trigger new insights for you. Shakespeare's plays can be interpreted and visualized in multiple ways, and there is no single correct meaning for any play or speech. The best interpretations are the ones that help you understand the text and which help you to explain what is happening in a play and why.

The Additional Resources section in the back of this book suggests some further ideas for reading, viewing, and writing about Shakespeare films. There are many ways to study film, from a formal standpoint, through the lenses of critical theory, or in the context of popular culture. The approach you take will be shaped by your own prior experience with film and by the context of your class and the perspectives it provides.

We would like to add one note of explanation. Three of Shakespeare's genres are covered in *Screening Shakespeare*: the comedies, the histories, and the tragedies. Of the scholarly genre known as the romances (and, sometimes, also the tragicomedies) this book has almost nothing to say. There is a reason for this: cinematic films of the romances are very few and rather far between. Of *Cymbeline* and *Pericles*, we have only the BBC/Time Life versions dating from the early 1980s. Of *The Two Noble Kinsmen*, we have no version at all. *The Winter's Tale* offers a little more: three versions of the play (1968, 1981, and 1998). All, however, are straightforward film versions of stage productions, and only the two most recent are available on DVD. *The Tempest* has been treated far more frequently than the other four romances. It was reworked as science-fiction space epic, *The Forbidden Planet*, in 1956. It was recreated by Paul Mazursky in 1982 as a contemporary fable about an architect and his failing marriage in *Tempest*. It was more narrowly, but still quite freely, filmed by Peter Greenaway in 1991 as *Prospero's Books*. All three of these reworkings deserve to be studied. Together, they do not a chapter make.

We'll finish with this thought: learning and having fun with Shakespeare should be interconnected processes if not identical terms; we hope *Screening Shakespeare* offers some ideas and strategies that enable you to better understand and enjoy both the films and the plays.

CHAPTER 1

Shakespeare on Film

*T*he *Internet Movie Database* lists more than 700 films based on or
adapted from the works of William Shakespeare. His plays have
been translated into film since its very infancy as a medium: The
earliest known Shakespeare film dates from 1899 and stars the
English actor Herbert Beerbohm Tree in a two-minute silent version
of a death scene from *King John*. Since that time, *Hamlet* has been
filmed more than 90 times, *Macbeth* 50, and *Romeo and Juliet* 40 times.
Shakespeare's plays have been filmed in more than 20 languages and
in at least as many different countries. The plays continue to be
adapted and reinvented in new settings and genres. Recent film
adaptations include *King Rikki*, a 2002 film advertised as
"Shakespeare's *Richard III* in 21st Century Los Angeles"; *O*, a 2001
adaptation of *Othello*, in which the main character is a star player on
the high school basketball team instead of a military general; and
Scotland, Pa. (2001), which rewrites *Macbeth* as a black comedy,
featuring Joe "Mac" McBeth, a fry cook with an ambitious wife who
prods him on to kill his boss in a plot to take over the local greasy
spoon.

It's hard to imagine any other author who has had such a long-
standing influence on Anglo-American and world cinema. By way of
comparison, novelist Charles Dickens has been translated into film
168 times; mystery writer Agatha Christie, 78. Stephen King, the
English language's all-time best-selling author, has also been adapted
for the screen 78 times, too. (These numbers are based on
information from *The Internet Movie Database*.) Even these well-known
and popular authors, then, do not even approach Shakespeare in
terms of their cinematic productivity. The popular English playwright
of the Elizabethan and Jacobean eras has had a highly successful

5

second career in our time as a screenwriter, sometimes credited and sometimes not.

Alongside the films themselves, we find a growing body of scholarly and critical work on Shakespearean cinema. (Recent critical works are listed in the Additional Resources section at the back of this book.) Most of this scholarly output has been published since 1994, which shows that the study of Shakespeare on film remains a young and informal subfield within Shakespeare studies. However, one significant book in the field, by Jack Jorgens, did appear as early as 1977. There may still be some debate about whether Shakespeare on film counts as a legitimate element of Shakespeare studies, but it is clear that a growing number of scholars are taking film seriously as a medium for teaching and interpreting the plays. Performance theory and cultural studies have helped shift attention from the texts toward performance and popular culture as well as providing a rationale for continued serious study of the films.

What can we discover by taking the time to watch, discuss, and write about movies based on Shakespeare's plays? What can we get from a film that couldn't better be learned from sustained study of a play's printed text? Why, if you already have to read and analyze a dozen or so new plays in a semester, might you want to spend even more time watching four *Hamlet* films, two *Romeo and Juliet*s, and a brace of *Merchants of Venice*?

Our first answer is that watching a film can help you better understand what's going on in the text of a play. It's often difficult to read the printed text and visualize what's happening during a given speech or scene. The subtext is sometimes hard to judge, so a film provides a sense of setting, dramatic action, and context that can supplement a close reading of the text of a play. In a film, you can see the actors' expressions, read their nonverbal cues and body language as they speak (or listen, or react), and begin to see the dynamics of their relationships and the conflicts that drive the plot. Sometimes, students of Shakespeare can get bogged down by trying to interpret the sense of a line or scene and lose sight of the plot or the dramatic context. Watching a film of the same scene can help you see and hear what's happening and how events fit into the larger dramatic patterns of the play, even if you still don't know precisely what the lines mean. Hearing and seeing a good actor recite a speech can provide meaning in the form of tone, inflection, rhythm, and gesture that will help you get more out of the words when you return to the text.

What we know about the history of Shakespeare's plays suggests that they were written primarily for performance rather than for publication. Today, they lead a double life—in print and in performance—yet it remains likely that many readers have never seen a Shakespeare play performed on stage. If you have an opportunity to see live theatrical performances on campus or at a local Shakespeare festival, do so. There's no substitute for live performances to bring the plays to life. However, it's unlikely that you'll be able to find live performances for every play you want to read and study. So, the films, on DVD, provide a viable alternative. They can help you see how a play might be performed, how its setting might look, what costumes the actors might wear, what kind of music might accompany the dramatic action, what lighting effects could be chosen, and so on.

If you're studying Shakespeare in a formal college course (as we imagine most of our readers are), you're probably aware of an important tension between different ways of approaching Shakespeare. In his own lifetime, Shakespeare was entertainment— and commercial entertainment at that. He wrote the plays to be performed by professional acting companies, and these companies would stage the plays to audiences who paid to see them. He wrote for diverse audiences that would often include the educated (nobility) and the illiterate (peasants, or "groundlings") at the same performance. That's why we often find crude slapstick humor mixed with high-flown philosophy and poetry in Shakespearean drama. He tried to put something for everyone into his plays. In that sense, his plays are analogous to modern film as popular and commercial entertainment. (Of course there are significant differences between small-scale theater in the Elizabethan or Jacobean eras and big-budget Hollywood productions today, but these do not disqualify the analogy.)

Somewhere between 1616 and college, Shakespeare was reinvented as "literature." A study of how this happened is matter for a book or several books, but as a student in a college-level Shakespeare course *you* are participating in the continual production of Shakespeare as literature. You read the plays in a large and painstakingly edited anthology with footnotes and editorial apparatus that "frame" the plays as literary texts. You write papers, presumably, and get graded on your work. Eventually, you'll have credit for a Shakespeare course on your college transcript. Think about what that means for a moment. Shakespeare, more so than any other author in the English language, has come to signify a certain kind of education and cultural privilege which are connected to the problematic term "literature." Taking a course in Shakespeare has come to mean something in our culture, beyond the literal meaning that one has read and understood a certain number of the plays (and probably a few poems as well). It means one has access to certain (undefined) cultural values, ideals, and aspirations.

As your English professors will tell you, the term "literature" can be understood in many different ways, and it has been contested and redefined since the 1960s by a range of new schools of thought, including feminist criticism, new historicism, performance theory, postcolonial theory, and cultural studies. Nonetheless, the term "literature" still does have interpretive value, and no discussion of Shakespeare can avoid engaging critically with the debate over the meaning and significance of literature as cultural discourse.

So, watching a Shakespeare film in the context of a college-level literature course provides an occasion for looking critically at the value of literature, its relationship to popular culture, and the meaning of "Shakespeare" as a cultural icon. "Shakespeare" is both a myth and an industry. He is a myth in the sense that readers and critics over the years have created a persona to attach to the name "William Shakespeare" in order to account for the existence of the plays and poems for which they have such great affection. (More accurately, there are in fact several different competing versions of this persona depending on which critic or school you look at.) This persona has little to do with an actual person named William Shakespeare; it is primarily a creation based on interpretations of the texts. Nonetheless, people, including in this context filmmakers and directors, invest physical and emotional resources in this persona and create works of art informed by it. Shakespeare is also an industry, a critical industry which keeps many scholars, literary critics, and publishers busy; but it is also a broader cultural industry which involves tourism (in places like Stratford-upon-Avon in England and Stratford in Ontario, Canada), summer Shakespeare festivals, and—of course—films.

To some degree, any Shakespeare film necessarily engages Shakespeare as both myth and industry. The fact that it is identified as a Shakespeare film in the first place means that a whole range of expectations and ideals are going to be applied to such a film, whether consciously or not. A film can't *not* participate in the Shakespeare industry, nor can it avoid offering some kind of perspective on the myth of Shakespeare as author. As critical viewers, we can consider how a particular film participates in, resists, or even re-invents the myth of Shakespeare. Does the film present a "reverential" attitude towards the play and its author? Does it offer critical, playful, or even parodic views? Often a film may do both: it may include moments of reverence alongside moments of camp. Rarely are films one-dimensional or without internal contradictions in their stance and approach to Shakespeare.

On the one hand, there is an expectation that any film based on a Shakespeare play will stay "true" to the "original" (leaving aside the question of what those terms mean) and to capture and respect the depth and seriousness of the literary text. On the other hand, film is entertainment, and filmmakers must find ways to make the plays enjoyable and accessible for viewers who have not studied the plays before, either extensively or at all. These filmmakers can't assume, for example, that their audiences know the plot or that they have had experience listening to actors speaking in Shakespeare's early-modern English. This tension between Shakespeare as high art and Shakespeare as popular entertainment runs throughout the large body of Shakespearean cinematic work that has been produced over the past century and more.

The good news is that the tension between entertainment and literature (or art) continues to make Shakespeare on film interesting and important. While some films may be more serious and literary and others more entertaining and playful, any particular film will be both to some extent and occasionally at the same time. Like any cultural text, it will be marked by internal contradictions. How we interpret and evaluate a film will depend on our framework of analysis and interpretation for any particular play.

From Play to Film

Henry V, one of Shakespeare's greatest history plays, opens with a speech by the Chorus that offers an important commentary on both the powers and the limitations of the stage. The language of this speech is worth looking at in detail, in part because it offers a somewhat unexpected perspective on the *limitations* rather than the powers of stage drama as a mode of representation. After we've looked at the passage itself, we'll turn to two contrasting film versions of this same scene. The first, from Laurence Olivier's 1944 film of *Henry V*, offers a plausible view of what a performance at the Globe theater in Shakespeare's own day might have looked like. We can explore some of the stage conventions Shakespeare would have used and think about the experience of watching one of the plays performed in its original context. The second, from Kenneth Branagh's 1989 film adaptation, does for film what Olivier does for the stage. Branagh uses the opening Chorus to take us behind the scenes of modern filmmaking and, so, offers a rich contrast to Olivier's historical representation of Elizabethan theater. Taken together, the two scenes can help us consider some of the major differences between the stage and the screen.

Here is the speech delivered by the Chorus at the beginning of *Henry V*:

> O, for a Muse of fire, that would ascend
> The brightest heaven of invention!
> A kingdom for a stage, princes to act,
> And monarchs to behold the swelling scene!
> Then should the warlike Harry, like himself,

Assume the port of Mars; and at his heels,
Leashed in like hounds, should famine, sword, and fire
Crouch for employment. But pardon, gentles all,
The flat unraisèd spirits that hath dared
On this unworthy scaffold to bring forth
So great an object. Can this cockpit hold
The vasty fields of France? Or may we cram
Within this wooden O the very casques
That did affright the air at Agincourt?
O, pardon! Since a crooked figure may
Attest in little place a million;
And let us, ciphers to this great account,
On your imaginary forces work.
Suppose within the girdle of these walls
Are now confined two mighty monarchies,
Whose high uprearèd and abutting fronts
The perilous narrow ocean parts asunder.
Piece out our imperfections with your thoughts:
Into a thousand parts divide one man,
And make imaginary puissance.
Think, when we talk of horses, that you see them
Printing their proud hoofs i' the receiving earth.
For 'tis your thoughts that now must deck our kings,
Carry them here and there, jumping o'er times,
Turning th' accomplishment of many years
Into an hourglass—for the which supply,
Admit me Chorus to this history,
Who, Prologue-like, your humble patience pray
Gently to hear, kindly to judge, our play.

(Prologue 1–34)

This passage combines two traditional ways of beginning a work. The first, the invocation to a Muse, is a common convention of epic poetry: "O, for a Muse of fire." The Muse being invoked here is warlike, epic, heroic, a Muse "of fire." For only such a Muse could help "warlike Harry [King Henry], like himself, / Assume the port of Mars." Only with a "kingdom for a stage" would there be enough room to represent adequately the events of Henry's glorious victory over the French at Agincourt. The second tradition is the direct address to the audience. In this prologue, the Chorus serves as narrator by framing the story for the audience and asking for patience with the technical imperfections of the show. This narrator's address to the audience is a common device extending back thousands of years to classical Athenian tragedy.

What's important here is the way the Chorus describes the limits of the stage. He says, in effect, that the events of this story are simply too big to be rendered effectively with the available resources in a little theater such as the Globe. To his question, "Can this cockpit [the stage] hold / The vasty fields of France?" we implicitly answer, "No, it can't—at least not literally." We recognize that no live stage performance can show us what the siege of Harfleur or the battle of Agincourt really looked like. The "Muse of fire" would be able to show us the true face of war and the heroism of King Henry V at his moment of triumph; but alas, this Muse is nowhere to be found, and we are left instead with a crammed "wooden O" (the Globe theater itself, which was round) and the "unworthy scaffold" of the stage.

So, the Chorus has to ask us to use our imaginations to transform a little theater into the battlefield of Agincourt in order for the players to "dare" to present on stage the historical events of young King Henry's reign. As the audience for this spectacle, we are going to have to agree to play along by using our "imaginary forces" to transform one actor into "a thousand parts," "Turning th' accomplishment of many years / Into an hourglass" (the length of time it will take to watch the play).

Think about how this issue changes when we move from stage to screen. With the technology and the resources of modern filmmaking, it *is* in fact possible to re-create battles and sieges, to stage huge historical re-enactments with hundreds of horses and thousands of soldiers, and to film the whole event. Films like *Braveheart* or *Gladiator* clearly demonstrate the possibilities of re-creating quite convincing images of medieval or classical warfare. Using a combination of live action and special effects, the technology of cinema can extend our field of vision into dimensions that an Elizabethan or Jacobean dramatist would not have been able even to imagine. So what do you do with the Chorus and this opening scene if you're a director making a film instead of producing a live theatrical performance?

In his 1944 film, Laurence Olivier's answer was to film the opening prologue as a historical re-creation of a live stage performance as it might have looked on May 1, 1600—in Shakespeare's own time. (This date appears on a poster shown as part of the opening credits of the film.) The film opens with a wide shot of an elaborate model of London in 1600. The actual model constructed for the film was, impressively, about 50 by 70 feet in size. The camera pulls back: it moves out over the Thames from the Tower of London towards London Bridge before settling over two similar theater-like buildings along the south bank of the river. The camera teases us by hovering over the first theater-like building (which turns out to be the bear-bating arena) and then descending into what we now recognize as the Globe. It descends just as a flag is raised to signal the day's performance.

The scene shifts to the interior of this theater as we watch the patrons milling around and settling into their seats. Vendors are hawking fruit and ale, and as the camera pans around the little arena we get a very realistic glimpse of just what the Globe might have looked like moments before a performance of one of Shakespeare's plays. Some of the audience is ranked in tiered seats around the perimeter, and the "groundlings" stand immediately at the foot of the stage. A few wealthy patrons are treated to stools on the edge of the stage itself.

An actor playing Shakespeare wearing thick reading glasses takes a stool at the far left of the stage, where he will serve as prompter for the actors. He then signals to the conductor to start the music. A young boy carrying a signboard comes out with a sign announcing the title of the play, and then the Chorus takes the stage to loud applause. Presumably the man is a well-known actor, and the audience greets his appearance on stage warmly. It's not until seven minutes into the film that we hear the first spoken words: "O, for a Muse of fire."

Olivier's directorial solution to the film versus drama issue is clever: his film is actually a film of a play or, rather, a play within a film. He chooses to make Shakespeare's play itself the subject of his film. What we are seeing here is not *Henry V*, the film, so much as *Henry V*, a film of the play as it looked in Shakespeare's day. The most interesting moment comes about two-thirds of the way through the opening prologue when the illusion is itself broken. The actor playing the Chorus (Leslie Banks) actually steps toward the camera as it closes in on him, and he makes direct eye contact with the lens—it's as if he is breaking out of the frame of the play within the film to look directly at us, the audience of the film. This close-up happens just as he says "on your imaginary forces work"; he thereby makes the same appeal to us that Shakespeare's Chorus made to his live stage audience: Bear with us here, pretend, play along! Use your imagination and come with us on this great historical adventure!

As soon as this appeal occurs, the camera pulls back and the actor breaks eye contact. By doing so, he returns us to the feeling of watching from the upper balcony as the play takes place in 1600. There is only the one brief acknowledgment of our position as film spectators in this scene. At several points later in the film, however, Olivier will again play with the film versus stage distinction as he shuttles back and forth between theatrical and cinematic modes of presentation.

Forty-five years later, in 1989, Kenneth Branagh remakes *Henry V* as his first feature-length Shakespeare film. How does Branagh handle the opening scene? Branagh's approach is to take us behind the scenes of the film itself. His film opens not in the Globe in 1600 but on a cluttered sound stage where *Henry V* is being filmed. The prologue begins in complete darkness. The Chorus (Derek Jacobi) strikes a single match to illuminate his face as he begins the speech: "O, for a Muse of fire." He walks down a small flight of steps and then flips a large circuit-breaker to light up the scene. Immediately, we realize where we are: on a modern soundstage. The floor is littered with spotlights, camera equipment, candles, swords, banners, and other props. The back of the false walls reads "HV." Throughout the opening prologue, Jacobi speaks directly to the camera—and, by extension, to us as his film audience. It's almost as if he is playing tour guide taking us on a walk around the studio where Kenneth Branagh is hard at work on his new film, *Henry V*.

As Jacobi nears the end of the prologue, he moves toward a heavy set of medieval-looking doors. Just as he finishes his speech, "your humble patience pray / Gently to hear, kindly to judge, our play," he swings the doors open and the camera follows through into the darkness. We move with the camera from the frame of the Prologue into the story space of the film itself, and the main action of the film begins. As the film continues, Branagh, like Olivier, plays back and forth along the boundaries of the film and its frame.

Because they both work so self-consciously with the distinctions between stage and screen, these two opening sequences prompt us to think about the relationship between film and drama as ways of representing Shakespeare's plays. The translation of Shakespeare's works happens on two levels when they are made into films. First, the works themselves must be imagined and visualized as dramatic productions. The plays have come down to us through history as texts, of course; however, stage directions in Shakespeare are relatively few, in part because no Shakespeare manuscripts have survived and in part because Shakespeare himself probably worked directly with the actors and, so, didn't need to write directions down since he was there at rehearsals. Thus, the first "translation" happens when the text is transformed into live drama. Any dramatic production is already an interpretation of the play itself.

A second translation follows when the drama is filmed: Now, a director has to make decisions about not only how to *stage* the play but also how to *film* it. Some of the films we will explore in more detail are relatively straightforward representations of the plays, produced more or less as retellings of the stories in a film environment. Others are more experimental or broader in their adaptations of the materials of the plays into film form. Richard Loncraine's *Richard III*, for example, moves the events of the play into a 1930s fascist environment with a lead character (played by Ian McKellen) costumed and made up to look suspiciously like Hitler. Julie Taymor's *Titus* takes *Titus Andronicus* (Shakespeare's bloodiest and most brutal play) into the world of postmodern spectacle by setting it in a strange theatrical universe that blends medieval costumes with motorcycles and backs it all up with a punk-rock attitude.

What Olivier's and Branagh's work with the opening Prologues shows us is that the relationship between film and theater is complex, multidimensional, and fluid. A film, as Olivier shows, can enclose within it a stage production. Just as Shakespeare often uses the device of the play-within-the-play to dramatize the relationship between art and life, so too can film directors create a parallel device using the play-within-the-film. As Branagh demonstrates, it's also possible to take Shakespeare's concept and adapt it in order to create a film-within-a-film. His *Henry V* repeatedly uses the devices of the chorus and the frame to look at the mediated nature of historical representation and to pose questions about the nature of heroism, war, and epic for contemporary audiences.

Analysis and Interpretation: Henry V *'s opening sequence*

1. Watch the opening sequence of both versions of *Henry V*. Pay particular attention to the way each film takes viewers "backstage." How do these films represent the mechanics of stage and film production?

2. Many films try to make the relationship between the audience and the story as invisible as possible. Such films try to make us forget that we are watching a film that has been constructed to create the illusion of reality. By contrast, Shakespeare's plays often self-consciously remind us that theater is an illusion or a game. So do these two films. Make a list of the specific ways in which each of these opening sequences breaks the illusion to remind audiences that they are watching a film. How do these devices change your relationship to the story? How do you respond to such a breakage?

From Script to Screenplay

Like *Henry V*, *Romeo and Juliet* begins with a Chorus who serves as a narrator to the story by providing background information to help the audience understand what it will be watching. Here's how the Chorus begins:

> Two households, both alike in dignity,
>> In fair Verona where we lay our scene,
> From ancient grudge break to new mutiny,
>> Where civil blood makes civil hands unclean.
> From forth the fatal loins of these two foes
>> A pair of star-crossed lovers take their life. . . .

The Chorus quickly tells us that this story is located in Verona, Italy; that two rival families of high standing have an ancient grudge that has once again broken out into new conflict and bloodshed; and that the children born to these two warring families are fated to be "star-crossed" in their love.

In a stage performance, it's quite likely that the Chorus would simply walk out to the front of the stage and deliver this speech to the audience directly. Then he (or she) would step aside or pull back a curtain to begin the play's opening fight sequence. How might this be handled in a film? Baz Luhrmann's clever solution in his 1996 film, *William Shakespeare's Romeo + Juliet*, is to transform the Chorus into a television-news anchor. By intercutting, Luhrmann intersperses segments of the anchor's speech with segments from the opening fight scene, so he moves back and forth between exterior shots of the fight scene in Act 1, Scene 1 (set in a gas station parking lot) and the choral prelude shot in an interior (a television studio).

Here is the opening sequence, as it appears in the screenplay by Craig Pearce and Baz Luhrmann:

EXT. HIGHWAY. AFTERNOON.
A ribbon of freeway stretching into a blue and pink late afternoon sky. A huge dark sedan, windows tinted gold, powers directly for us.
CUT TO: A heavy, low slung pickup truck traveling toward the sedan.
WIDE SHOT: Sky, freeway, the cars closing.
TIGHT ON: The sedan.

TIGHT ON: The pickup.

Like thunderous, jousting opponents, the cars pass in a deafening cacophony of noise.

INT. TRUCK. AFTERNOON.

TIGHT ON: The fat face of GREGORY, yelling at the disappearing sedan.

GREGORY

A dog of the house of Capulet moves me!

He and the pimply-faced front-seat passenger, SAMPSON, explode with laughter.

The red-haired driver, BENVOLIO, keeps his eyes on the road.

INT. TV STUDIO. DAY.

An ANCHORWOMAN; behind the faces of two middle-aged men. The caption reads, "Montague; Capulet. The feud continues."

She speaks to the camera.

ANCHORWOMAN

Two households both alike in dignity.

(In fair Verona, where we lay our scene)

From ancient grudge break to new mutiny,

Where civil blood makes civil hands unclean.

EXT. GAS STATION. AFTERNOON.

The truck is in the busy driveway of a large gas station, being filled with gas. The surrounding walls are painted with murals of blue sky and palm trees. (1–2)

Most of what we read here is description of each scene or shot (camera position) as visualized by the director. The position of the camera is recorded for each scene: Cuts, wide shots, and tight shots are described for every segment of the film. In all, only *five* lines from the play itself appear here (Gregory's taunt to the passing Capulet car, and the first four lines of the Chorus). The rest of the space is taken

18

up with specific description of the scene as visualized by the director and screenwriter.

Luhrmann creates a sense of visual tension and drama by cutting quickly back and forth between the fight scene at the gas station and the news anchor's report of the renewed violence. The rest of the lines of the Chorus are spoken as voice-overs several pages later. In Luhrmann's version, the events play out on the screen simultaneously with the narrator's framing for the audience.

Even this brief excerpt from a screenplay suggests how much work goes into transforming the text of a Shakespeare play into a screenplay for a film. Screenwriters and directors have to think about each scene and each shot within that scene: where to set it, what the actors should look like, where the camera is positioned, how and when the lines are delivered, and so on. Usually, a screenplay will serve as the basis for a set of storyboards. From such storyboards, an even more detailed shooting script is developed before filming can begin.

If you've studied film before, or worked on a film yourself, you will understand the labor-intensive process that is required to go from a story (or play, or idea, or concept sketch) to a finished film. And filming itself is only part of the process. After filming is complete, editing and post-production crews go to work transforming hours and hours of film footage into a carefully sequenced series of scenes that will work for audiences. They also add sound, music, effects, and so forth.

It can be quite useful, particularly if you are writing an essay on a film (or films), to have a copy of the screenplay or to create one of your own. You can create your own "scene outline" for specific sequences to describe the way each scene is setup and filmed (as we will do later in this chapter). This strategy can help in understanding the complex structuring process used to transform the text/script of a play into a dynamic visual medium.

Experiencing Drama and Film

Let's take a step back at this point and consider some of the differences between attending a live theatrical performance and watching a film. A live theatrical performance is an immediate, living event. We are physically present in a time and place with the actors who are speaking and moving about the stage in a choreography of bodies. Their presence and their direct interaction with the audience lend a dynamic interchange to the event. Fed by the audience's laughter, it is often the clowns and the comic characters that steal the show. The comedies, especially, come to life on stage in a way that can be hard to replicate on film (let alone on the page). The verbal humor, puns, and physical comedy can be hard to get from the text of the play in silent reading, but in live drama the action and life can be breathed back into the play in surprising and delightful ways.

Because of the large space of the theater, the actors have to project their voices in a live performance. We become accustomed to exaggerated voices and gestures; even asides and whispers must sometimes be shouted out, especially in the large outdoor theaters where summer Shakespeare festivals are frequently presented. For soliloquies, the convention is usually for the actor to step towards the edge of the stage and to address the audience directly. Even though he is projecting a loud stage voice, we understand and accept that Hamlet, for example, is "thinking to himself" as he wonders whether or not to commit suicide. Just as there is no equivalent of a close-up shot in a live performance, there's also no voice-over or dramatic interior monologue. We simply accept that the soliloquy represents such an inner debate or conversation.

In a theater, our point of view is generally fixed. Unless we switch seats or watch from backstage, we are more or less stuck in place as we watch the show from our seats. The space of the stage is a bounded space, and we view it from a single, stationary point of view. While we have the freedom to focus on whatever we like, we generally do so within a fairly defined frame of vision. Within this visual space, the movement of the actors' bodies can itself have a kind of choreographic effect. Characters can huddle together at the center of the stage; they can run off in separate directions as an alarm sounds. Their spatial relationships can be used to create dramatic tension: One actor may be looming over another or be up in a balcony; actors may be positioned on the stage to suggest conflict (through distance or visual hierarchy); they can move towards or away from one another; and so on. Yet, throughout these, our perspective is more or less fixed in place, and it is the actors and sometimes the sets that alter position.

In the cinema, our point of view is markedly different. It goes with the camera. We can move in very close to overhear whispered confidences between two actors, or we can pull way back to see an entire battlefield from miles away in the distance. We can roll around a scene (as when the camera is mounted on a dolly) with our viewpoint moving dynamically to see events unfold from a changing perspective. However it is handled in a particular film, the camera *mediates* our relationship to the actors in a film by inserting a crucial distance between us and the performers, a distance not present in live drama. Some directors may use a relatively fixed camera to create a viewing experience which is more like watching a play; others may move wildly about the space of the film with a highly dynamic camera in order to create effects and experiences that are radically cinematic as well as different from, and impossible to achieve in, a live play.

Sound and audio effects can also work quite differently in a film. Soliloquies can be done as voice-overs, where a character is heard speaking but is not necessarily talking out loud or addressing us directly. The convention of the filmic voice-over is now so familiar to us that we assume an off-screen voice represents thinking rather than talking. Filmmakers can use this convention to great advantage when adapting some of the major scenes and speeches in a play for the screen. Combined with the mobile camera, the use of audio and voice-over can enhance our experience of the psychological overtones in Shakespeare's drama. For example, a voice-over can be combined with imagery so as to place us, metaphorically, inside the characters' minds. In addition, film can be used to amplify such interior monologues in a way that can be hinted at but not directly represented in a live performance.

In place of live theater's immediacy, film offers us a more edited construction. The director has tighter control over our attention (we see only what the camera shows us) and can also use editing techniques and other devices to construct an experience for us. In watching a film, at least on DVD, we can always pause, go back, or move forward, and thus re-experience the film in ways even its director could not have intended.

The common element linking the films we'll explore with live performance is—above all—the language. With very few exceptions, the films we'll discuss in *Screening Shakespeare* stick to Shakespeare's scripted language and do not attempt to translate Elizabethan or Jacobean idioms into contemporary speech even as they nearly all use excerpted or edited versions of the texts of the plays. One notable exception to this generalization is Kenneth Branagh's *Hamlet*, which does use the complete text of the play (with a few minor edits *and additions*), and which runs for more than four hours as a result. The scenes and the historical contexts may be changed, sometimes radically, in some of the films, but the lines being spoken by the actors are still those that were written by Shakespeare.

Beyond the language, the stories themselves are usually the same and survive the translation into film. Hamlet still despises his stepfather and worries about his wavering mother. Lear's daughters still fight over the inheritance. These stories may be plotted and represented differently on film, but they are still in a meaningful sense the same stories. Rather than speak of live performance and film as completely distinct, separate categories, we'll view them here in a more complex relationship, as we've seen in the example of the Prologue to *Henry V*. Instead of an absolute divide between theater and film, many of the examples we'll discuss in these pages play on the fact that there is a continuum between drama (live) and cinema (mediated). As critical viewers and informed readers of the plays, we can learn much from the interaction of dramatic and cinematic elements in the major films.

Analysis and Interpretation: The Viewing Experience

1. Make a list of key differences between attending a live stage performance and watching a film. If you've recently gone to a

Shakespeare performance, try to capture as many details as you can remember. How is your involvement in a play different from your experience of a film? How does the experience of film change as you move from the large screen of the cineplex to the smaller TV?

2. Shakespeare plays often have speeches (soliloquies) designed to represent a character's inner thoughts. How have you seen this handled on the stage? What different techniques have you seen in films to represent a character's thoughts?

3. Can you think of specific plays or types of plays that would be better in live theater than on film? What are the advantages of live drama for each genre (comedy, tragedy, history, and romance)?

Three Approaches to Studying Shakespeare Films

Whether we're watching a film for enjoyment or for educational reasons, we're always using some kind of framework or theory. Even the idea of watching a film purely for entertainment is itself a crude or unvoiced kind of film theory. When we turn to films based on Shakespeare's plays, our first point of reference is most likely going to come from our prior experiences with Shakespeare. Our experience of a film will be different if we know a play well in contrast to watching a film of a play we've never read. In our own case, we have taught *Hamlet* often and had seen five film versions of the play before watching Michael Almereyda's *Hamlet* (featuring Ethan Hawke as Hamlet) for the first time. we could in a sense only interpret that film in the context of our own extensive history with the play. This history meant that we couldn't avoid interpreting Almereyda's film as a commentary on earlier film versions as well as an attempt to produce a distinctly contemporary or even postmodern version of the play. In contrast, having taught it only a couple of times we were not as familiar with *Titus Andronicus* the first time we watched Julie Taymor's *Titus*, so we found myself asking a different set of questions about the play and Taymor's interpretation of it. We were less sure about what Taymor had created and what came from the Shakespeare play.

Film as Literary Adaptation

Since we're analyzing films in the context of a Shakespeare course rather than, say, a film-history course, our first point of reference will always be the texts of Shakespeare's plays. In a film-history course, we might choose to look at Laurence Olivier's *Hamlet* (1948) in the context of other psychological thrillers of that time period (thrillers which popularized a style known as *film noir*). Instead, our focus will be on Olivier's *Hamlet* in comparison to other filmed *Hamlet*s as they wrestle with the meaning of Shakespeare's play. The literary context provides our first framework for analyzing the films.

Think about the kinds of decisions directors such as Olivier and Branagh had to make as they composed scenes—the Prologue to *Henry V* that we looked at earlier, for example. Initial questions might have been whether to film the Prologue at all or whether to include the Chorus as a character in the film. Since the purpose of the Prologue is to ask the audience to use its imagination to transform the stage into an epic battlefield, it might be redundant for the films actually to show the battles taking place (as they both do) since the audience for the film would then be able to see those things the original spectators couldn't have. It's quite possible either director could have edited the Prologue out and moved directly into the action of the play by beginning with the debate over the legitimacy of Henry's claim to France. Why didn't they do it that way? Why did both Olivier and Branagh decide to keep the figure of the Chorus, begin with the Prologue, and "frame" their films using the dramatic device of the Chorus and his direct address to the audience?

Questions such as these can be discovered in almost every moment of a Shakespeare film. Screenplays rarely follow the text of the play exactly: characters may be edited out, combined, or revised in some way; entire scenes may not be included or new material may be added. (In the case of *Henry V*, both Olivier and Branagh include brief flashbacks to Henry's earlier friendship with Falstaff when they used lines that from *Henry IV*, *Part 2* the previous play in the historical sequence.

The first time you watch a film, it may be best just to sit back and watch to get a feel for how the film works. Such a first viewing is often called a "participatory reading," a process that can be applied to reading a literary text on the page as well as viewing a film. On a second viewing, however, it's helpful to follow along with the text by marking the lines that are included and getting a sense for the outline of the script. You will notice patterns in how the play's text is edited, shaped, and crafted for presentation on screen. This type of reading is often called an "analytical reading" in order to indicate that you are moving from participation to analysis by breaking a film down into its components for closer study.

One useful practice in analytical reading is to develop a scene outline, where you make note of each scene in the film and its corresponding lines in the play. Here's an excerpt from a scene outline we created for Michael Almereyda's *Hamlet*.

1. [0:00] Open on a view of NYC towers through the back window of a limousine. Legend reads: "New York City, 2000 / The King and C.E.O. of Denmark Corporation is Dead / The King's widow has hastily remarried his younger brother / The King's son, Hamlet, returns from school, suspecting foul play . . ."

2. (2.2) [0:52] Times Square: Hamlet walks across the street to his room at the Hotel Elsinore. In his room, recorded on his personal video player, we see grainy B&W images of Hamlet himself, speaking: "I have of late . . . lost all my mirth . . . ./ What a piece of work is a man. . . ." (These lines appear in Act 2, Scene 2.) His phone rings. On the screen, images of animal skeletons, the Gulf War, and a B-2 bomber taking off. "And yet to me what is this quintessence of dust?"

3. [2:35] Title screen (blood-red background)

Each numbered section corresponds to one scene or continuous sequence in the film. Usually there are clear breaks between scenes (fades to black, dissolves, or some other film technique), but sometimes you simply make arbitrary decisions to break a sequence of shots into a numbered scene. There's no *right* way to do this; the purpose of a scene outline is to help you get a sense for the shape and structure of the film. Use whatever method makes sense to you for a given film. Above we have outlined the first three scenes, making up a total of about three minutes of screen time.

The numbers in the square brackets refer to the time of the film, beginning at 0:00 and running sequentially through each scene. (You can get this number from your DVD player very easily. It helps to track how much screen time is devoted to each scene.) The numbers in parentheses represent the corresponding act and scene numbers from Shakespeare's play. In this case, it's interesting to note that Almereyda presents parts of Act 2, Scene 2 (2.2) *before* Act 1, Scene 2.

For each scene, provide a brief description of what is presented on the screen while paying attention to how each image is framed and composed as well as who is doing and saying what. Breaking down a film and annotating it in order to create a scene outline such as this helps to understand how a particular film adapts the text of the play. It also helps to see the extent to which the film is a constructed, formal artifact, a carefully and artfully produced assemblage of individual shots. Remember that any performance, dramatic or cinematic, necessarily has to make certain interpretive decisions about the play.

Influenced (perhaps unconsciously) by Shakespeare's status as cultural icon, many reviewers and critics approach films based on his plays in terms of how well or how "authentically" they represent the "original" play. In such an approach, Laurence Olivier might be criticized (as in fact he was by some critics) for adding a voice-over at the beginning of *Hamlet* or for not including the Fortinbras subplot. As interesting and helpful as it can be to compare a film with the literary text on which it is based, it's important to resist the impulse to assume that Shakespeare's text represents some ideal to which a given film has to live up. In a sense, *adaptation* is not exactly the right word to use here because any film is itself a performance or reinvention of the play and is more actively engaged in constructing meaning than the rather passive term *adaptation* might suggest.

This observation is especially true in the case of Shakespeare. As you probably know, no true "original" or hand-written text exists for *any* of Shakespeare's plays. The scripts that you read in your textbooks are edited reconstructions based on historical and textual scholarship performed on printed editions, and the location of lines, the spelling and meaning of words, the stage directions, and many other details continue to be the subject of intense debate. Even an edition of a Shakespeare play is itself already a kind of performance. We simply do not know *exactly* what Shakespeare meant to say.

Consider that a filmmaker may be working from a different edition of the text, and that he or she may hold a very different interpretation of the play than the one with which you are familiar. The meaning that is created in and by a Shakespeare film is perhaps best seen as a dialogue with the text of the play rather than an adaptation. A film in a sense talks back to the play by placing it in a new and different context and by reworking its language to produce what is often a very different and even unexpected meaning.

Film as Art Form

As you begin to analyze the ways a film works with the text of a play to shape and present it for the screen, you come to recognize the importance of film form and strategy in the creation of a cinematic experience for viewers. The study of film as an art form is a discipline in its own right, and if you have never taken a film course or studied film in an academic setting, some of the terms and concepts may be new to you. (In a Glossary at the back of this book, we've defined film terms we use.) A particularly valuable resource for students and film enthusiasts is David Bordwell and Kristin Thompson's *Film Art: An Introduction*, a book that is widely used as a text for undergraduate film courses. We'll refer to that book as a resource often, especially for its definitions and illustrations of formal techniques in film.

The opening sequence of a film is especially important: it introduces viewers to the world of the film; it guides us into the space of the film and its story; it sets up certain expectations about where we are and what that place is like. In the example of the two *Henry V* films we looked at earlier, we can see two different strategies at work.

The Olivier film almost immediately announces itself as a historical re-creation, from the choice of type font used in the credits to the elaborate model of London that is the first image presented on screen. The opening sequence is framed as a film about a play being performed live at the Globe Playhouse in 1600.

We are situated by the film as a member of the live audience seated in one of the upper tiers of the house. By the time the Chorus takes the stage to speak the opening lines, we already understand that we are watching a play within a film. We expect certain things as a result, so the film can play with those expectations to create a sense of drama and surprise. When, for example, Leslie Banks moves toward the camera for a close-up, looks directly "at us," and says "on your imaginary forces work," we feel we are being directly addressed. At the same time, we are reminded that we are experiencing a film and not a play. Olivier continues to make use of this surprise as his scene eventually does shift from the reconstructed Globe to Southampton and then on to the fields of France.

The Branagh film self-consciously places us squarely in the middle of the world of filmmaking. As Derek Jacobi wanders through the sets and props, we are reminded that films are not magic; they are crafted and acted and edited and built by people through a very labor-intensive, collaborative process. Branagh's opening sequence echoes Olivier's in its use of the prologue, but for Branagh it is important to frame the tale not in terms of the stage but in terms of the craft of film. We see Jacobi standing there with a camera in the foreground, and we cannot help but remember that film, like theater, is an illusion—a game in which we willingly participate.

The world created for us by the opening of a film creates expectations that the film may later use, modify, or subvert in some way, but those first few moments establish the vital relationship between the viewer and the film. Once we have entered into the story-world of a film, we can study it for its production design. What kind of a world has this film presented to us? *Hamlet*, for example, has been filmed in several very different kinds of settings: in a dark, foggy medieval castle isolated from the world; in an eighteenth-century country house, a world of spectacle and lavish beauty; in a modern but nondescript hotel; and in contemporary Manhattan, where the characters carry laptops but speak Elizabethan English. Set design, location, and *mise-en-scene* all work together in a film to create this fictional cinematic world.

A film may establish a surreal, mystical landscape (like Kurosawa's *Throne of Blood*, his version of *Macbeth*), or it may create a very realistic landscape such as contemporary New York City. The creation of this film world is a crucial part of the language of a given film: it is to the filmed story what set design and costuming are to live theater. In both cases, the visual elements of the setting help to create a specific environment that works on us at both literal and emotional levels.

In approaching film on a formal level, we also pay attention to the camera: How is it positioned? Is it moving or static? The camera serves as the audience's eyes in a film, and it's important to pay attention to where the director and the cinematographer are guiding our gaze. There are many different types of camera angles and movements, and we'll define and discuss most of them in context as they arise. We'll also often want to attend closely to the role of the camera in creating the film as we experience it.

Notice, for example, the importance of the camera's movement in the opening of Olivier's *Henry V*: It begins with a very wide shot of the cityscape of London, and then takes us on a visual tour of the city in 1600 before closing in and descending from a high vantage point (an aerial view) into the space of the Globe theater itself. We enter the world of the theater from a great distance then, and the effect is to create a sweeping, epic context for the opening moments of the film. By contrast, Branagh's camera begins with a very tight shot on Jacobi's face lit by a single match. The effect is more claustrophobic—we begin in total darkness. Then the camera's gaze follows the Chorus through the crowded and cluttered sets backstage before exploding into the world of the film itself. We move with the camera through a set of heavy doors into the space of the film's story, and the overall effect is more dark, enclosed, foreboding than is Olivier's opening sequence.

An additional layer of formal analysis comes from a study of the way a film is edited. Editing works closely with the camera to create the feel of a film. The editing establishes a rhythm and pacing for the film: Are there lots of long takes, or many short shots spliced rapidly together? Is the scene interrupted by many edits and new camera angles, or do we stay with a particular shot or vantage point for an extended time? A filmmaker such as Baz Luhrmann tends to use rapid-fire editing to create a breathless, visually chaotic, and startling effect on viewers. Laurence Olivier generally employs slower pacing, an effect that tends to draw us more deeply into the psychological subtext of brooding characters such as Hamlet.

Music and sound provide additional layers of interpretation that we'll want to pay attention to as we look at specific films. Music creates a mood in a film, and recurring songs or themes can serve to develop sound links or sound bridges from one scene to another or to echo an earlier moment in a film. Sound effects and other audio used in a film also create formal meaning in specific ways. Almereyda's *Hamlet*, for example, uses video and digital footage within the film to create a voice-over narration for some of Hamlet's speeches. Rather than hearing Hamlet speaking directly, we hear his grainy, recorded voice instead. The film poses important questions through that use of sound about the way human relationships are now mediated by technology.

Like the beginning sequence of a film, the ending also carries special weight. As you analyze a film for its formal construction, pay attention to the way it ends. Closing images often leave the most powerful and lasting impression on an audience.

Film as Cultural Text

When we analyze a film as literary adaptation, we look for its meaning primarily in relation to the literary texts and traditions with which it engages. In our second framework, we shift to a new context by considering how a film uses the conventions, forms, codes, and devices of cinematic art to produce meaning in the context of other films. Our third interpretive strategy or framework shifts to yet another context. Here, we look at film in the broader context of culture, a focus which raises two vital questions: What in this context do we mean by culture? How does this view shape our understanding of film?

The meaning of the word *culture* has shifted and expanded over the last few decades as scholars in several disciplines, including women's studies, history, anthropology, semiotics, media studies, and literature, have worked to challenge the notion of culture as exclusively the domain of high art and class status. This new understanding shifts the definition of culture from something one *has* (or does *not* have) to something one *does*. If you think of culture in the narrower, traditional sense of the word, you are likely to imagine artistic forms such as ballet, opera, and perhaps even Shakespeare plays. People who are "cultured" participate in these events and gain access to certain kinds of power and prestige as a result. Our newer definition of culture, however, is not restricted to this class-specific understanding. Instead, we now tend to define culture as a way of life: a process we use to negotiate our way through everyday life, make sense of what's happening, and assign meaning and value to a wide range of texts, events, and objects.

Culture in fact is a system of codes and strategies that we use to make meaning in a nearly infinite number of ways. We can only begin to understand and make sense of events and daily life when we have a context to which we can relate them, and in this sense culture is that which provides these contexts for understanding who we are and what we're doing. For example, think about your own experience as a college student. That experience is mediated through a whole host of cultural codes of different types. The way you understand and experience the identity of "college student" is a result of your use of and interaction with these codes. One rather clichéd code is college as an "ivory tower," a place one goes to get away from the immediate and practical demands of life to think and study. Sometimes this code implies that college is a waste of time—impractical, and detached from the "real" things that matter. Some college professors are viewed by students as aloof, detached, or out of touch, a symptom of the power and persistence of the code of college as ivory tower. A different cultural code suggests college as youthful celebration, a place for frat parties and late-night revelry. (A whole book could be written about the films that rework this cultural tradition, from *Animal House* to *Old School*.) A third code signifies college as a route to a better career and a better life. We might call this the code of college as upward mobility. All of these cultural codes, and many others, structure and filter your experience of "college life" every day.

Exploring the cultural discourses linked to the identity of "college student" might not provide much insight into a Shakespeare film (although it's worth remembering that Hamlet himself is a non-traditional college student at the beginning of Shakespeare's tragedy!). However, there are other cultural codes that undoubtedly do produce significant results. Take, for example, the issues of gender and sexuality. Feminist literary critics were among the earliest readers of Shakespeare to demonstrate how the plays reproduced the cultural assumptions about men and women and the relationships between them that were typical of Elizabethan and Jacobean England. By shifting the analysis from Shakespeare as literature to Shakespeare as cultural text, feminist scholars were able to demonstrate the complex relationships between Shakespeare's representations of gender and other non-literary representations of gender in legal codes, property ownership, popular culture, religion, and so on.

We can make a similar interpretive move with film. By looking at the representations of women and men—femininity and masculinity—we can explore how these films both participate in and sometimes critique or disrupt the dominant codes and discourses of modern patriarchy. This disruptive relationship is usually a complex matter. Rarely is an individual film either purely "sexist" or purely "feminist" in its representations of gender and power. It is almost always the case that a mainstream feature film will to some extent reproduce the dominant codes and ideologies of its own times. In order to appeal to an audience large enough to support the costs of making a feature film, filmmakers need to produce films that appeal to their audiences, which means that films tend to reproduce some or most of the dominant culture's expectations and values. This observation may not always be true of small-budget or art-house films, which aim to be aesthetically and culturally disruptive. (Derek Jarman's *The Tempest*, for example, foregrounds homoeroticism in ways that might well offend some mainstream film audiences.) Most films offer moments where they subvert (or come close to subverting) dominant representations of gender and power, just as they have moments that reproduce those dominant codes. The point is to explore the contradictions and complexities.

Like feminist literary criticism, feminist film theory has developed into a discipline in its own right over the past four decades. Feminist film theory started out by looking at the way women were represented in film. Did film offer positive images of independent women? Did film offer women alternative ways to experience femininity and female sexuality outside the domain of patriarchy and consumer culture? From there, feminist film theory has evolved in several directions. Feminist theorists explore the power of "the gaze": Who is looking? Who is being looked at? How does a film position its viewers as spectators? Are we assumed to take a "male" position as we watch? What would a female or feminist viewpoint look like in film? Feminist film theory draws extensively on Freudian and post-Freudian theories of sexuality with theories of spectatorship and subjectivity developed from French poststructuralism, as well as the work of feminist filmmakers and screenwriters around the world. It's a rich and complex field, and this description doesn't even scratch the surface. There's a great deal of work to be done in Shakespeare film studies by scholars and students who want to use a feminist lens on the work of filmmakers.

Gender differences are not the only issue that come to the forefront when we look at film as cultural text. Culture is where meaning and power intersect, and just as gender is one specific node in the matrix of power and discourse so, too, are race, social class, sexuality, and ethnicity parts of a field of cultural and linguistic difference. Some of Shakespeare's plays address issues of racial and ethnic difference explicitly: *Othello* and *The Merchant of Venice* come to mind as plays in which race and ethnicity figure as principal elements of the plot. But even plays and films that do not at first appear to focus on race or ethnicity can be interpreted and analyzed for their representations of such differences (or their apparent silence on the subjects). Social class figures prominently in many of the plays and can be a subject for analysis as well. The point in analyzing film from a cultural perspective is to look beyond the surface to consider how the language, imagery, and formal elements of the film construct relationships of power and meaning at virtually every moment.

Shakespeare, as we discussed earlier, remains a powerful cultural force: as a highly literary author and as a cultural myth or icon. In taking a cultural approach to Shakespeare films, we are less concerned with how adequately those films represent the plays and more interested in considering how they can be interpreted in the context of contemporary culture. Shakespeare films circulate and compete in a densely populated cultural landscape. To a certain extent, they are part of popular culture as much as literary culture or literary history. As you watch a film such as Baz Luhrmann's *William Shakespeare's Romeo + Juliet*, you might want to think about how it compares to other love stories you have seen on film. What kind of meaning can you discover in the way Luhrmann's film plays with conventions of teenage love and romance? What about the religious symbolism? How do Catholic and Latino cultural references add to the layers of meaning? How does it change your understanding of Tybalt to see his character played by John Leguizamo? Questions such as these and many others can be generated when we approach films as cultural texts. There is almost no limit to the ways in which Shakespeare films can be interpreted when you place them in the context of contemporary culture.

Questions for Analyzing Films

This checklist is intended to suggest some of the lines of inquiry you might take when adopting each of the three frameworks or interpretive strategies discussed in this chapter. These questions are meant to be suggestive rather than exhaustive. Use them to generate your own questions. Return to this list as you consider specific films. Add, modify, or adapt questions. Develop more refined approaches.

Film as Literary Adaptation

✓ How much of the play's text is used in the film? How is the text of the play edited, cut, reorganized, or rewritten within the film? On which version of the text is the screenplay based?

- ✓ On which characters does the film focus? Are certain characters given more (or less) emphasis in the film than in the play?

- ✓ How are key scenes and speeches in the play presented in the film? Does the film seem to offer any specific interpretation of the meanings or motivations of characters' actions and words?

- ✓ How is the language of the play supported by the acting, visual elements, and editing of the film?

Film as Art Form

- ✓ How does the film begin? How are viewers introduced to the story world of the film? Where are we positioned as spectators? What expectations are established in the opening sequence?

- ✓ How do the location, set design, costuming, and other elements of *mise-en-scene* create a fictional world? How would you describe the visual setting or environment? What effect does it have on the mood and tone of the film?

- ✓ How is the camera used? Is it mobile or static or a combination of the two? Does the camera stay close in or move back to a distance?

- ✓ How does the editing create rhythm and continuity in the film? Is the pacing slow or fast? Are editing techniques used to create tension or contrast?

- ✓ How does the film end? Where are viewers left at the close of the film? Are we given any retrospective distance from the story? Is the narrative "framed"? Does the ending offer a sense of closure?

Film as Cultural Text

- ✓ When was the film made? What social and historical contexts does it seem to be responding to, explicitly or implicitly? What about the film seems dated? Why? What seems current or contemporary? Again, why?

✓ How does the film reinterpret the themes of the original play into a contemporary context?

✓ How are relationships between men and women presented? Does the film rely on conventional definitions of masculinity and femininity? Does it offer any contrasting or unconventional views of gender and gender difference? What kind of power do men possess and use? What kind of power do women possess and use?

✓ Are there any nonhuman characters in the film (witches, fairies, mythical creatures, gods and goddesses, ghosts)? How are these characters presented? How do they interact with human characters? What kind of language and imagery is used to describe them? Do these nonhuman characters seem to have a gender? A racial or ethnic identity? What function do these characters serve in the film?

✓ Does the film present any religious or cultural images or icons (crosses, cathedrals, cemeteries, temples, or masks)? How are these images or icons used in the film? What do they signify? How are their meanings changed, or at least influenced, by the events of the story?

✓ Which characters in the film are marked or identified by their social class or economic status? Are any characters unmarked by class difference? Does social class have any relationship to power in the film? Do any characters move from one class to another? How?

✓ Does the film echo or allude to other cultural texts (other Shakespeare texts, other literary texts generally, other films, popular culture, or music)? How are these "intertexts" significant in the film?

Questions for Writing and Discussion

1. Create your own list of differences between film and live drama. Think back on plays and films you've been to and how those

experiences affected you as a viewer. What strikes you about the nature of the two different art forms? In what ways are film and drama similar? Do they create similar feelings and responses in their audiences? What social or cultural purposes does each serve?

2. Take a favorite scene from one of the plays you've been reading recently and look at it through the eyes of a film director. Think about how you would film the scene for a movie on which you are working. What kinds of decisions would you have to make? How would you approach the scene differently if you were producing it for a live performance in a theater?

3. Watch the opening sequence of a film version of one of the plays you are currently reading in class. (Consult the filmography in the Additional Resources section at the back of this book to help identify relevant films available on DVD.) Make note of as many film-specific moments as you can: Are there places where the camera moves? Close-up shots? Voice-overs? Create a list of the techniques and devices used in the film that would not be possible in a live performance.

4. Take one of the plays you are reading and imagine you are the casting director for a new film to be made based on the play. Whom would you choose to play each of the roles? Why? How did you make your choices? What criteria did you use in selecting the cast? How would your film change with different actors?

CHAPTER 2

The Comedies

I t's a common joke that all of Shakespeare's comedies end with weddings (or the likelihood of weddings) and all his tragedies with funerals. While this joke may not be literally true, it is indeed the case that many of the comedies end on a note of celebratory closure, one marked by a wedding or festival. No matter how complicated the conflicts may have become during a Shakespearean comedy, the ending will nearly always be marked by a sense of resolution and a return of order. Some of these resolutions may strike modern audiences as contrived or unrealistic—too many things have to fall into place for characters to get out of their self-imposed, messy situations—but, nonetheless, the comic plot almost always tends towards the reassertion of order and stability. Of all the major genres in which Shakespeare wrote, comedy is his most formulaic.

Comic Form and Structure

It's often quite useful, when coming to terms with one of Shakespeare's comedies for the first time, to divide its story into three parts. The first part is an expression of the initial order in his fictive world. The second part disrupts this order by means of some force, dilemma, person, or conflict. The third part usually features the return of order by a resolution of the conflict or disruption. Some of Shakespeare's later "problem" comedies do not fit this model, but most of the early- and middle-period comedies do. This tripartite structure is a somewhat crude and schematic way to view the plots, but it can be a useful starting point for analyzing filmed versions of the comedies.

In his classic text *Anatomy of Criticism*, literary critic and genre theorist Northrop Frye describes comedy as "the mythos of spring" and outlines comic structure as follows:

> What normally happens is that a young man wants a young woman, that his desire is resisted by some opposition, usually paternal, and that near the end of the play some twist in the plot enables the hero to have his will. In this simple pattern there are several complex elements. In the first place, the movement of comedy is usually a movement from one kind of society to another. At the beginning of the play, the obstructing characters are in charge of the play's society, and the audience recognizes that they are usurpers. At the end of the play the device in the plot that brings the hero and heroine together causes a new society to crystallize around the hero. . . . The appearance of this new society is frequently signalized [sic] by some kind of party or festive ritual, which either appears at the end of the play or is assumed to take place immediately afterward. (163)

Frye's theories have been criticized for several reasons. Feminists have argued that his model privileges male heroes and ignores the specificity of gender differences in many of the works he analyzes; historicist critics have demonstrated that his archetypes are ahistorical and do not allow for social context or patterns of change over time in the literary genres. So, we're not suggesting that we adopt Frye as an overarching framework for the analysis of Shakespeare films. What we would argue, however, is that Frye's model of comic structure can help us to see the larger elements and plot dynamics that operate in many of the comedies on film.

In *A Midsummer Night's Dream*, for example, the initial order consists of the world of the Athenian court: its laws and authority. This authority is represented by the figures of Theseus (the Duke of Athens) and Egeus (a member of the ruling class and father to Hermia). Egeus's authority is challenged by Hermia, who resists the arranged marriage preferred by her father. She wants, instead, to marry Lysander, to whom she is emotionally and romantically attached. Theseus intervenes on behalf of Egeus and the patriarchal authority he represents by invoking a law that says Hermia must accept her father's choice of a husband or be punished by death or isolation in a convent. So, the initial order is one of patriarchal authority and established rules. The complication or disruption that challenges this order is romantic love and desire, represented by the affection between Hermia and Lysander.

In order to escape the laws of their Athenian elders, the young lovers run away to the woods outside the city. Most of the central action of the play takes place in these woods, a fictive world not ruled by law or patriarchy but by the mischievous fairies, by desire, and by dreams. After a confusing, dream-like night in the woods (which the lovers may or may not come to remember), the lovers are welcomed back to Athens by Theseus, who has been convinced to overrule Egeus's demands and allow the lovers to marry as they wish. Order is restored at the Athenian court, but in this case it is a *new* order, signified by the joint wedding of three couples, an order which successfully incorporates romantic love and desire with the original law and order of the state. In effect, our third phase is a fusion of the first and second. The Athenian court authority is re-established, but it has been softened and humanized by the experiences of the young lovers, whose disruptive desires are successfully incorporated back into society.

Think about how the play *might* have ended differently. Hermia and Lysander could have run off into the woods and never returned; they could have lived out a different life under the sign of the fairies and their world of fantasy, dreams, and desires. Conversely, Hermia could have been scared by her night in the woods and gone back to admit that her father was right all along. She could have accepted his choice for her husband: Demetrius. Neither of these things happens of course, and Shakespeare instead presents a comic resolution that blends elements of both worlds.

We can see the three-part structure quite clearly in the imagery, costumes, and settings of filmed versions of *A Midsummer Night's Dream*. Costumes and settings for the opening scenes are generally formal and signify wealth and prestige. Once we journey into the fairy world of the wood, however, the look and feel is completely different. The formal world of the court is replaced by shimmering moonbeams, lush overgrown vegetation, and costumes that are brightly colored, fantastical, and linked to nature rather than to culture or city. When we return to Athens at the end of the play, the setting and imagery usually combine elements from both the court and the wood to symbolize the fusion of the two worlds.

Comedy depends on leaving audiences with a sense of closure and rightness, a feeling that things have turned out as they should. Often there are interesting issues left unresolved or whisked away by the rapid *dénouement* in the comedies. These are worth looking at as well. How much does Katharina really believe her own speech about wifely obedience at the end of *The Taming of the Shrew*, for example? How much do young lovers remember about their midsummer's night in the woods? Does Hermia recall that Lysander has turned on her and humiliated her for being short and dark haired? Does Helena remember chasing Demetrius around like his "spaniel"? Shakespeare's comedies continue to resonate with audiences because of their ambiguities and subtexts. Indeed, Shakespeare brilliantly manages to have it both ways in his comic plots: he weaves a perfectly contrived happy ending for his audiences, but only after venturing far into potentially tragic situations and leaving some vital issues unresolved or open to re-interpretation. Contemporary filmed versions of the comedies succeed to the extent that they recognize and bring forth these ambiguities, ambiguities which mirror real life for all of us.

Analysis and Interpretation: Comic Form and Structure

1. Use Northrop Frye's generic plot outline to examine the plot of one of Shakespeare's comedies. Who is the protagonist or hero? (There may be more than one.) What obstacles stand between him (or her) and his (or her) goal or desire? How are these obstacles overcome? Who helps or hinders the protagonist? Why?

2. What kind of society is established or re-established at the end of the play? Has the original society or state been changed or overthrown? By whom? How? Why?

3. Consider the relationship of setting to plot. Is there a division between a civilized or cultivated world and a primitive wood or fantasy world? How are these differences represented in the play? Who journeys into the fantasy world? Why? How are they changed by their experiences there?

4. Many of the comedies use multiple plots. Make a chart or table to identify the main plots and their relationships to each other in the play on which you are working. Which characters are linked to or contrasted with others? How are these characters different from each other? How may the characters be grouped together?

The Comedies on Film

The comedies have not been nearly as popular among filmmakers as the tragedies. However, they do remain immensely popular nevertheless, and they are frequently performed on the stage. In part, this preference for live action may be the result of the comedies often working better in front of a live audience. Many of the comedies include physical humor, verbal banter, and staged movements (such as dances) that are hard to re-create in a film. With few exceptions, the great directors have favored a steady diet of tragedy, especially *Hamlet, Othello, King Lear,* and *Macbeth.* Fortunately for our purposes, however, there have been several reasonably successful films made of the major comedies. Not only are the comedies significant in their own right, but they also foreshadow some of the themes and characters that Shakespeare would return to later in the great tragedies. In the next several pages, we'll be looking chronologically at a range of Shakespeare's comedies, from one of his earliest (*The Taming of the Shrew*) to one of his last (*Twelfth Night*) with stops along the way at *A Midsummer Night's Dream, The Merchant of Venice,* and *Much Ado about Nothing.*

The Taming of the Shrew

The Taming of the Shrew is one of Shakespeare's earliest comedies, composed in 1590 or 1591. It is also one of the first Shakespeare plays ever to have been produced as a Hollywood "talkie" (or sound film). In 1929, Sam Taylor adapted the play for the screen and directed Mary Pickford and Douglas Fairbanks Sr. in a sophisticated, successful film. Taylor cut the Induction from the play along with most of the Bianca—Lucentio plot. He did so in order to focus on the relationship between Petruchio and Kate (played by the real-life husband and wife team of Fairbanks and Pickford). At the time, the two were Hollywood's biggest box-office draws, and their fame certainly contributed to the film's success for United Artists. A restored version is now readily available. It's short (only 66 minutes) and contains only about 25% of Shakespeare's text, but it's a rare treat nevertheless. There are other more or less faithful film versions of the play, too. In the first category, there's the American Conservatory Theater version, produced in 1976 and starring Fredi Olster, Marc Singer, and Stephen Schnetzer. In the second, there's the well-known Liz Taylor and Richard Burton vehicle, directed by Franco Zeffirelli and released in 1967.

The Taming of the Shrew also forms the basis for a recent teen film, *10 Things I Hate About You* (1999). Directed by Gil Junger, *10 Things* stars Julia Stiles as Kat, refigured as a post-feminist intellectual whose bad experiences with boys have led her to swear off dating. The film's Petruchio, "Patrick Verona," is a troubled hunk from Australia played by the late Heath Ledger. While the film is only loosely adapted from Shakespeare's play and the language is rewritten as modern dialogue, *10 Things* does show the continuing resilience and adaptability of the *Taming* story for contemporary audiences. If you plan to write about *Taming of the Shrew*, it may be worthwhile to rent *10 Things I Hate About You* as well as the 1929 version (or the later iterations of 1967 and 1976). Lacking Shakespeare's original language, *10 Things* doesn't help much with an understanding of the text of the play itself, but it is interesting to consider what it says about the continuing relevance of controlling fathers as well as misrepresentation as a strategy for getting a date. The charged gender politics of Shakespeare's original plot continue to resonate even when the setting for *Taming* is moved to the contemporary suburbs. (We discuss *10 Things* in more detail in Chapter 5.)

Zeffirelli's *The Taming of the Shrew* (1967)

Continuing the tradition established by Sam Taylor's high-wattage casting, another famous real-life husband and wife team, Richard Burton and Elizabeth Taylor, appeared as Petruchio and Katharina in Franco Zeffirelli's 1967 film version of *Taming*. Their star power alone was enough to propel the film to some degree of success— Zeffirelli's *Taming* would inspire a renewal of interest in Shakespeare on film and inaugurate a second major period of productivity in the late 1960s and early 1970s. The first major period, in the late 1940s and early 1950s, was fuelled by Laurence Olivier and Orson Welles. Audiences in 1967 would have been unable (indeed, wouldn't have *wanted*) to separate the on-screen and off-screen dramas of Burton and Taylor, whose stormy relationship often made headlines. For viewers at the time, Burton *was* Petruchio (his well-documented drinking just adding drama to the picture) and Taylor *was* Kate. Audience responses to the plot and dialogue undoubtedly would have been colored by their feelings about the stars in the lead roles. More than 40 years later, our response to Zeffirelli's film can be more detached and critical, and we're in a better position to make critical inquiries into the film's take on the central issues of gender and power.

Watching Zeffirelli's film today, viewers come away with many of the same questions audiences and critics of Shakespeare's play have been debating, seemingly forever. To what extent is Kate actually "tamed" by Petruchio? Is her transformation into spokeswoman for domestic obedience (in her closing speech at Bianca's wedding feast) for real, or is she "playing along" with the game to help Petruchio win his bet? Has male authority triumphed over resistant femininity? Or have Kate and Petruchio "fallen in love."? Although Zeffirelli transforms some of the verbal banter of the lead characters into physical comedy for the screen, his screenplay stays fairly close to Shakespeare's original script. As you think about how you respond to and interpret

Kate's words and actions at the end of the film, you'll want to go back to the text of the play to look more closely at her lines and their implications. Certainly, Petruchio uses both physical and psychological violence on Kate to persuade her to change her behavior. The brutality of his tactics is inescapable, and the film does not shy away from dramatizing this violence. To what extent has Petruchio whipped the spirit out of Kate? How self-conscious is her transformation? Has she just learned how to play the game? Is her apparent obedience to patriarchal convention really a sophisticated form of resistance?

Despite the power and appeal of Burton and Taylor, we shouldn't overlook the importance of the Lucentio—Bianca plot. Shakespeare often uses multiple plotting to reflect on a central theme or motif from several points of view. Remember that Petruchio's courtship of Katharina is motivated by money (he knows he'll get a dowry of 20,000 crowns as well as inherit half of her father's lands). The theme of marriage for money appears as well in the Bianca plotline. Bianca's father insists on a signed contract from Lucentio's father before he consents to their marriage. Identity and disguise are also strongly presented themes in the Bianca story since all of her suitors are forced at some point to woo her in disguise in order to penetrate her father's defenses. The noble Lucentio appears to Bianca as a struggling language tutor. In a reversal of the *Joe Millionaire* story, Lucentio is able to reveal to Bianca that he really is wealthy after all, a son of the Pisan aristocrat Vincentio. Shakespeare's frame tale in the play's Induction would seem to suggest that it's easier for a rich man to get away with playing poor for a while than for a poor man to pretend to be wealthy.

In an ironic reversal, Zeffirelli seems to suggest that the fair Bianca may have been playing at docility as much as her older sister, Kate, has been playing the shrew. We're left wondering in the final scene if she has been duping Lucentio all along since he apparently has begun to wonder as much himself. Identity, appearance, convention, money, and gender create the plot's complications, and not all of the strands are completely tied up in the film's fast-paced *dénouement*.

Zeffirelli's set design and art direction feature a carnivalesque element: Just as Lucentio arrives in Padua, a carnival begins, and throughout the film the town is convulsed by celebration and partying. This carnivalesque eruption creates an environment of misrule and parody in which social conventions are mocked and challenged. The street scenes evoke a *mélange* of Mardi Gras and the Day of the Dead and create a vibrant and ironic subtext that calls into question the power and authority of the legitimate leaders (the fathers). While the comic closure of the play *seems* to put things back in order, Zeffirelli's subtext leave some of these key questions less clearly resolved than the play's ending lines might suggest.

Analysis and Interpretation: The Taming of the Shrew

1. Why do you think Zeffirelli chooses not to include Shakespeare's Induction? How might the Christopher Sly frame story be filmed? What would its inclusion add to the film? Would it change the way audiences respond to the two main plots?

2. How does Zeffirelli use the Lucentio—Bianca plot to amplify and complicate the themes of the film? Does his use of Shakespeare's multiple plotting add to your understanding of the main issues in the film? How are Lucentio and Bianca different from Petruchio and Kate as they are portrayed in the film?

3. What evidence is presented in the Zeffirelli film to suggest that Katharina is joking or commiserating with Petruchio when she delivers her famous speech on obedience at the end of the play? Would you argue that she has been "tamed"? Or is something else going on in her relationship with Petruchio?

4. Some commentators have described the relationship between Kate and Petruchio in this film—as portrayed by Burton and Taylor—as "a childish tug-of-war for power" (Welsh, Vela, and Tibbetts 93). Others have seen a more balanced and viable marriage of wit and passion. What evidence for each view do you find in particular scenes? Which of these two views would you favor? Why? Or would you describe the relationship in different terms?

46

5. Zeffirelli's *Taming* has been credited with re-establishing the viability of Shakespeare for a wider film audience and with generating a second renaissance of Shakespeare film in the late 1960s. In addition to the use of superstar actors, what elements of this film do you think contributed to its popularity at the time? How do the setting, art design, and costuming of the film contribute to its mass appeal?

A Midsummer Night's Dream

A Midsummer Night's Dream is frequently performed at summer Shakespeare festivals and remains one of the most popular of the comedies. The contrasting worlds of the Athenian court and the fairy wood allow for exuberant costuming and set designs, and the magical and playful themes make the play an enduring favorite with audiences. The comic plot includes two pairs of young lovers, an authoritarian father who disapproves of his daughter's choice in love, and a journey into the wood to escape the rule of law and patriarchy. After a series of confusions and misadventures in the wood, things are all sorted out satisfactorily in the end with three linked wedding ceremonies taking place at the court of Theseus, Duke of Athens. Act 5 focuses primarily on a play-within-the-play as the newlyweds are treated to a crude performance of the love story of "Pyramus and Thisbe" put on by Bottom the weaver and a company of tradesmen or "rude mechanicals."

As in so many of the comedies, *A Midsummer Night's Dream* has several layers of meaning. It rewards deeper analysis. Beneath the surface of enchanting magic and comic confusion, the play touches on several themes that connect it to the later comedies as well as to some of the tragedies. Any film or stage production wrestles with critical questions about how to interpret and present these themes. First, consider Duke Theseus and his relationship to his bride, Hippolyta. While we know Theseus and Hippolyta are about to be married, we also know that the Duke has won his wife by defeating her on the battlefield: "I wooed thee with my sword," he says, "And won thy love doing thee injuries" (1.1.16–17). Hippolyta is herself, then, literally one of the spoils of war, and Theseus reports having defeated her on the battlefield. She is both his prisoner of war and his fiancée. Queen of the Amazons (the legendary tribe of women warriors), Hippolyta has to have some seriously mixed feelings about her subjugation as wife and hostage. Actors and producers have to decide what form her resistance, if any, might take.

The subtext of male power and authority runs through the stories of the young lovers as well. All four are portrayed as utterly conventional types and in many productions the two men, Demetrius and Lysander, are presented as essentially interchangeable. The women, Hermia and Helena, are usually distinguished only by height and hair color (since both are referred to in the text of the play): Helena is usually tall and blonde, Hermia short and dark. None of the four is especially deep, so we are given little motivation for the preference in love which each expresses.

The lovers' night in the wood becomes the occasion for some of the more disconcerting subtext to surface. As Helena chases Demetrius through the wood in 2.1, she presents herself in a pose of complete abjection: "I am your spaniel . . . / The more you beat me the more I will fawn on you" (203–204). She seems to invite and welcome both mental and physical abuse in these lines. In Act 3, Lysander, under the spell of the love potion, turns on his lover Hermia and professes that he hates her. He even contemplates killing her. "What, should I hurt her, strike her, kill her dead?" he says. "Although I hate her, I'll not harm her so" (3.2.269–270).

While the four lovers do get sorted out and reconnected by morning, audiences are left to wonder how much of the emotional and physical violence of the night before remains to affect them. The play seems to suggest that love is both powerful and fickle and that passion includes elements of power, possession, and violence alongside romance and kindness. Are the four lovers in any way transformed by their experiences in the woods? Do they remember anything of that night? The text of the play does not deal explicitly with these questions, but film and stage performances have opportunities in the way they present Act 5 to bring up some of these unsettling questions.

The power struggle between Oberon and Titania, King and Queen of the Fairies, frames the story of the human couples. Oberon and Titania are feuding over custody of a "changeling boy," and their fighting has caused chaos in the natural world by upsetting the weather and the cycle of the seasons. Oberon concocts his revenge in the form of the love potion that causes Titania to fall in love with Bottom the weaver, who has himself been magically "translated" into a half-human monster with the head of an ass. As Oberon tells Puck in 4.1, the plot works, and Oberon wins the boy through his mischievous magic. As with the other male—female relations, we see the role of power and illusion at work. When she awakens, Titania asks for an explanation as she gazes upon Bottom's long-eared form: "How came these things to pass?" (77). Oberon's only response? "Silence awhile" (79). Oberon asserts that the Athenians will be no more affected by their misdeeds in the wood than by a bad dream: "May all to Athens back again repair, / And think no more of this night's accidents / But as the fierce vexation of a dream" (4.1.66–68). However, dreams may be more powerful than he would like to admit.

A fourth subplot accompanies the "rude mechanicals" and their play within the play. While Theseus and the Athenian couples largely dismiss "Pyramus and Thisbe" as a mindless, clumsy distraction, the play as a whole suggests otherwise. The world of the stage is artfully linked with the world of magic and dreams. It is as if the theater is a gate between the waking world and the fairy wood, a kind of pathway for imagination, dreams, revelry, and even magic. In *Dream*, the stage is a space upon which the erotic and psychic energies of art and romance may find their way into the more mundane world of the waking audience. Puck's closing speech to the audience makes the link between the stage and the dream world explicit:

> If we shadows have offended,
> Think but this, and all is mended,
> That you have but slumbered here
> While these visions did appear. (5.1.418–421).

The play leaves us with quite a few questions and lingering thoughts about just how powerful and transformative the shadows and slumbers of the stage may be. Like a strange dream before waking, the play is not so easily shaken off.

A Midsummer Night's Dream: *Noble (1996) and Hoffman (1999)*

Two recent film versions of *A Midsummer Night's Dream* offer a wonderful opportunity to look at the different ways the play can be imagined and produced as a film. Adrian Noble directed a 1996 version based on the Royal Shakespeare Company's stage production. This film focuses more on the language of the play (as one would expect an RSC version to do), and it employs a relatively sparse set-design—in particular for the wood sequences. In contrast, Michael Hoffman's 1999 film of the play was produced as a Hollywood feature film and starred well-known film actors (among them Kevin Kline, Michelle Pfeiffer, Rupert Everett, and Stanley Tucci). So, it is quite lavish in its locations and set design. While the Noble film aims to adapt to film a production largely imagined for the stage, the Hoffman film clearly aims to translate *A Midsummer Night's Dream* into the language of Hollywood.

The Noble/RSC film adds one key element not originally a part of Shakespeare's play. The film opens in a young boy's bedroom, and we are expected to understand the main action of the story as *his* dream or nightmare. Not only is the film understood to take place in this unnamed boy's dream world, but he is also present throughout as a witness. At times the actors almost stumble over him, but we are apparently supposed to understand that he is invisible. To some extent, he represents the audience, encouraged by Puck to perceive the whole thing as if it were a dream. In another scene, he plays with the actors literally as his puppet show in a sequence that seems to equate him more closely with the playwright or director (pulling the strings, literally) than with the audience/dreamer. The heavily eroticized plot, especially the Titania—Bottom sex scenes, appear out of place, perhaps, in a young boy's dream. Nonetheless, the use of this device works to put an interesting spin on the relationship of drama and art to life.

The artistic direction of the Noble/RSC film blends elements of surrealism with more traditional stagecraft. One of the major motifs is the umbrella, which at certain times seems to come straight out of Mary Poppins (the fairies travel about using umbrellas as a form of magical locomotion) and at others to come from the surrealist imagery of painter René Magritte. The world of the fairy wood is a simple stage, bordering a lake and decorated with hundreds of bare light bulbs. These fairy/firefly bulbs are for the most part the only decoration on the stage, with the exception of the umbrellas and a few simple props. The simple imagery of the set suggests a non-localized dream world rather than a specific geographical place. Throughout, Noble uses doorways, false walls and doors, and other partitions to conjure up a surreal, two-dimensional place in the imagination, a nowhere that could be almost anywhere. Occasional special effects are used, however, to remind viewers that the film is to be understood as happening in the boy's dreams. Strange shifts in perspective and point of view, tilted cameras, and bright primary colors all contribute to this effect.

Despite its framing as a youthful dream, however, the Noble/RSC film includes in its script more of the unsettling and provocative lines than does the Hoffman version. The fairies are more eroticized, more devious, perhaps more threatening. The gender politics are foregrounded almost from the very beginning: Hippolyta slaps Theseus in the opening scene, so as to punish him physically for his authoritarian and heartless application of Athenian law. (Theseus has sided with Egeus and demanded that Hermia agree to marry Demetrius instead of Lysander or be punished with either death or banishment to a convent.) In contrast, the Hoffman film includes only a mildly scolding look by Hippolyta at Theseus in place of the more obvious slap in the face.

Michael Hoffman's film seems intended to introduce the play to a wider audience.. The actors include recognizable film stars Kevin Kline (as Bottom; Kline is actually an accomplished Shakespearean actor and has played Hamlet, among other major roles), Michelle Pfeiffer (Titania), Rupert Everett (Oberon), and Stanley Tucci (Puck). For viewers who know the play, a certain amount of the charm of this film comes from watching familiar actors play their sometimes miscast parts (Tucci as a balding fairy, for example; or Calista Flockhart as a continually exasperated Helena). Watching these performances in direct contrast to the RSC acting, one can see the distinctly different styles of voice and gesture in stage and film styles of acting.

Hoffman adds a bit of resonance and backstory to the character of Bottom. Kline's character is given a wife, who does not approve of his "dreaming" and his acting pretensions. He is an object of social ridicule: Two boys douse him with red wine as he rehearses in his white linen suit. Hoffman seems in this way to extend Shakespeare's insights into the world of the theater to offer the merest outline of a new subplot focused on Bottom and showing the consequences of choosing a life of stage acting and illusion over a life of practical affairs. Hoffman treats Bottom rather sentimentally in the film as an object of pathos, but his treatment of the character does contribute usefully to a way of thinking about the role of actors in the "make-believe" that comprises the theater.

There is one last surprise in the Hoffman film: how he presents the "Pyramus and Thisbe" play at the end. While the Athenian audience mocks the players by maintaining their sophisticated ironic poses, the actor playing Thisbe pulls off his wig and speaks as a man (out of costume now) and delivers the badly written lines so well that even Theseus (a man of experience) is visibly moved. This brief sequence extends some of Shakespeare's themes about the power of theater, for it turns out that this Thisbe is actually a fantastic actor, for he is able to move even the most jaded audience to tears through the sheer power of his acting.

In contrast to the Noble/RSC film version, the set design and locations for the Hoffman film are detailed and lush. "Athens" is actually Mount Athena, somewhere in Italy (backed by operatic music throughout); the fairy world of the wood is lush, Victorian, vegetative, and sensual. The film works very hard to realize the more fantastic illusions about what the wood and the court might look like. The luscious vegetation and neo-Victorian scenery is sometimes undercut by the slapstick bicycle chases, an effect which culminates in a completely over-the-top scene in which Helena and Hermia engage in nearly-naked mud wrestling. The foolishness and pettiness of "these mortals" is certainly brought forth in obvious ways in

Hoffman's film. Nonetheless, *A Midsummer Night's Dream* proves to work effectively as light-hearted Hollywood fare.

Analysis and Interpretation: A Midsummer Night's Dream

1. The Noble/RSC and Hoffman films use differently edited scripts of the play. In Hoffman's screenplay, one notable edit cuts the lines in which Theseus reveals that he has won Hippolyta as his bride by defeating her on the battlefield. What other differences do you see in the lines and scenes each play includes or deletes? What does each film choose to emphasize or diminish? Why? Which edited version of the play do you prefer? Why?

2. Adrian Noble's film adds an element not present in Shakespeare's play: the young boy who is both dreaming and participating in the events. How does this device change your relationship to the events of the film? How effective do you find Noble's additional element? Why would a director choose to portray the play literally as a dream?

3. Michael Hoffman gives a deeper presence and backstory to the character of Bottom. What does he add to Shakespeare's play in order to do this? How does the emphasis on Bottom and the "rude mechanicals" shift the thematic emphasis of the film?

4. Compare the acting styles in the Noble/RSC film with those in the Hoffman film. What differences in technique and presentation do you notice? Which techniques and styles are more effective on film? Why? How does the technology of filmmaking change the way actors present their lines and interpret their characters?

5. Adrian Noble's set design is minimalist compared to Hoffman's. What visual effects and props does Noble use to create his film's story world? Is his set and direction more appropriate or successful in presenting a dream world? How and why?

6. How does each of these two films address issues of gender and power? How does the mirroring of themes in the three different couples' plots work to suggest a particular view of the nature of

love and romance? Does either film challenge contemporary views of love and romance?

7. To what extent are Shakespeare's assumptions about the power of theater also true of cinema as well? Do either of these films comment, implicitly or explicitly, on the power of cinema to transform audiences?

The Merchant of Venice

What is remarkable about *The Merchant of Venice* is that it is a comedy at all. To achieve this feat and still allow the play to deal with the serious issue of anti-semitism, Shakespeare dispatches the marriage theme, essential to the comedies, by the end of Act 3. With Portia and Bassanio, Nerissa and Gratiano, and Jessica and Lorenzo married, the play can then showcase the trial scene at the opening of Act 4 before it brings back the marriage theme in darker hues with the comedy of the rings with which the play closes.

There is a very fine 1973 National Theatre production of the play available on DVD. It's directed by Jonathan Miller and stars Laurence Olivier as Shylock ("stars" is always the operative word when it comes to Olivier) as Shylock. There is a slightly later version (filmed in 1980 and featuring the veteran British actor Warren Mitchell in the role of Shylock). It is almost as good and also available on DVD. Where Olivier as the outcast Shylock tries by dress and accent to be more "proper" than those in power, Mitchell goes very much to the other pole by emphasizing Shylock's ethnicity at every turn. It is, however, to the 2004 feature-film version of the play that we want to devote our attention here. It's directed by Michael Radford and has Jeremy Irons in the titular role and Al Pacino as Shylock. The film shows what good direction, high production values, and inspired acting can achieve. It can't be definitive because the play itself is so controversial, but it can be—and is—worthy of detailed study.

Radford chooses right from the start to nail the setting to a particular date and place: Venice 1596. Having established that with the first frame, he then moves on to more screen writing as text scrolls and then fades. We learn some historical background about the exact way in which the supposedly enlightened and cosmopolitan Venetians persecuted the Jews. In our view, this dose of history doesn't work because it's too disruptive, but we can appreciate Radford's intent. He wishes to make clear right from the beginning that we should sympathize with Shylock. And since we think the play is about all religious intolerance (Christianity as much as Judaism), then Radford is justified in motivation if not in execution.

Then we are treated to an extratextual introduction of more than six minutes in which the major characters are made known to the audience, all of this happening even before we get to the opening line of Shakespeare's play. So, we have a scene in which the merchant, Antonio, spits on Shylock's clothes In this way, the director graphically illustrates Shylock's complaint to Antonio in Act 1, Scene 3:

> You call me misbeliever, cutthroat dog,
> And spit upon my Jewish gaberdine,
> And all for use of that which is mine own. (109–111)

He also has Shylock call out to Antonio so that we, as audience, know who the merchant is. Next, Radford indicates the hypocrisy of the Venetians by having them consorting with prostitutes even as they complain that Jewish usury is immoral. He then finishes this cinematic, atmospheric introduction with a nod to the other important characters: Antonio catches sight of Bassanio and affectionately murmurs his name; Lorenzo sees Jessica and sighs hers.

And so the play's text begins. Radford bravely uses Shakespeare's language even as he makes some pretty radical cuts and shifts scenes around to tell the story a little differently from the way it was originally told more than 400 years ago. The emphasis is now more on Antonio and Bassanio's relationship than on that between Bassanio and Portia. The latent homoeroticism in the original is made explicit as Antonio and Bassanio kiss each other on the mouth. The film ends with three memorable images that emphasize the price paid by the lead characters for their intransigence and their racism: first, we have Antonio left alone at Belmont as Portia and Bassanio leave (presumably to consummate their recent marriage); then, we have Shylock kneeling in the square, a broken, *Christian* man as the rabbi closes the door of the synagogue; finally, we have shots of a beautiful Belmont (Portia and Bassanio's estate). And then the credits roll. It's as if Radford is saying nature in all its beauty goes on even as humanity demonstrates (yet again?) its extraordinary talent for violence and unhappiness.

That last scene contrasts beautifully with perhaps the most arresting image in the film: a goat being slaughtered in the marketplace even as Bassanio and Shylock discuss the loan of 3000 ducats. Business is bloody is the message. Nothing good will come of the loan, except, of course, for the marriage of Bassanio and Portia. And even this hope is attenuated by Radford as he makes Bassanio's wooing of Portia seem even more mercenary than Shakespeare does, and Shakespeare himself ends the play by showing that Bassanio may not be that much of a catch. Having sworn never to give up his wedding ring, Bassanio gives it as a gift to Balthasar (Portia in her lawyerly guise). He can *say* to his wife:

> when this ring
> Parts from this finger, then parts life from hence.
> O, then be bold to say Bassanio's dead,
> (3.2.183–185)

But, he can change his mind with alacrity and without demur when his true love, Antonio, asks him to reconsider:

> My lord Bassanio, let him [Balthasar] have the ring.
> Let his deservings and my love withal
> Be valued 'gainst your wife's commandment.
> (4.1.447–449)

we would have liked a little less monkeying in this film with scene sequencing and a little less time spent on scene setting, but Radford's film *is* a serious effort to transfer Shakespeare to the screen in such a way that Shakespeare's ideas are brought out in a film that stands on its own merits. It's an effort of which Shakespeare would, we believe, have thoroughly approved.

Analysis and Interpretation: Radford's Merchant of Venice

1. One of the major arguments about *The Merchant of Venice* is whether it is a play about anti-semitism or an anti-semitic play. Examine a couple of film versions of *Merchant* (including Radford's). Do you discern a different position over this argument? What evidence can you find in each to support your conclusion?

2. Venice is one of the world's truly beautiful cities. How does Shakespeare make use of the setting? How does Radford? Would the play be the same if Shakespeare had set it in, say, Windsor (as in *The Merchant of Windsor*)?

3. Shakespeare's *Merchant* is oddly titled since the central character would seem to be Shylock. How does Radford treat the merchant, Antonio, whose profession constitutes part of the play's title? Is he more or less central to the action in Radford's film in comparison to the text of the play?

4. If the loan is one of the play's plots and the marriage of two of the principals another, how do Shakespeare and Radford treat a third: Jessica's elopement with Lorenzo and her apostasy? Given its connections with both the marriage and the religion themes in the play, does Radford use it as a bridging device, for example?

5. Some of the funniest scenes in the play are those involving the caskets and Portia's suitors, and in particular the Princes of Morocco and of Aragon. How does Radford stage these for maximum comic effect? Does he go beyond what the play intends? Why or why not?

Much Ado about Nothing

Much Ado about Nothing is one of a group of three romantic comedies written between 1598 and 1600. Along with *Twelfth Night* and *As You Like It*, *Much Ado* represents the acme of Shakespeare's festive comedies. It's energetic, wise, and entertaining. The play puts two romantic couples and their stories in dramatic contrast with each other. In one story, Claudio, a soldier who has done well in military service to Don Pedro, returns from war and turns his attention to finding a wife. His desire lights on Hero. Hero is the devoted and obedient daughter of Leonato, the Governor of Messina (the Sicilian city-state where the play takes place). The contrasting plot revolves around Beatrice and Benedick. Both have sworn to remain unmarried. Both adopt and maintain a pose of aloof nonconformity. Both profess cynicism about the opposite sex. Beatrice and Benedick are rich, fully developed characters (unlike many of the lovers in the comedies, who represent stereotypes), so the charged verbal exchanges between them form the center of the play's energy and drive its humor forwards. The "merry war" between them echoes back to *The Taming of the Shrew*, but in *Much Ado* the two characters are more evidently equal matches for one another. Power is balanced between them; the element of physical and emotional domination found in the earlier play (*Taming*) is missing. Its absence benefits the play.

As you might expect, both of these couples end up together (Claudio and Hero, Beatrice and Benedick), and, at the end of the play, plan to be married. As is generally the case in the plots of Shakespeare's comedies, the ending brings closure, re-establishes order, and manages skillfully to resolve the many conflicts and obstacles that have surfaced along the way.

So what are these conflicts and obstacles that come between the two pairs of lovers, and how are they overcome? In the case of Claudio and Hero, the obstacles to their romantic union come in the form of the rumors and false perceptions created by the play's villain, Don John, and his henchmen, Conrade and Borachio. They manage to mislead Claudio on two different occasions, and come very close to completely ruining his life—let alone his chances with Hero. On the first occasion, they convince Claudio that Don Pedro is courting Hero for himself rather than on Claudio's behalf. At the masked ball in Act 2, Don John talks to Claudio while pretending to think that he is speaking to Benedick. (The characters *are* wearing masks remember!) Claudio responds as Benedick, and Don John tells him that Don Pedro "is enamoured on Hero" and asks "Benedick" to "dissuade him from her: she is no equal for his birth" (2.1.158–159). Claudio's soliloquy shortly afterwards indicates that he has completely fallen into the trap by immediately believing the lie that Don Pedro is out for himself rather than trying to help his friend:

> Thus answer I in the name of Benedick,
> But hear these ill news with the ears of Claudio.
> 'Tis certain so. The Prince wooes for himself.
> Friendship is constant in all other things
> Save in the office and affairs of love;
> Therefore all hearts in love use their own tongues.
> Let every eye negotiate for itself
> And trust no agent; for beauty is a witch
> Against whose charms faith melteth into blood.
> This is an accident of hourly proof,
> Which I mistrusted not. Farewell, therefore, Hero!
> (2.1.166–176)

Claudio's willingness to accept false rumors about his friend Don Pedro (and to give up on Hero *very* quickly) suggests something close to a tragic flaw in him. He is quick to accept rumors of the worst, hasty in his willingness to abandon good faith and, instead, believe that people are base and self-serving at heart. Claudio's rush to judgment is of course contradicted by the facts just a few moments later. Don Pedro has won the heart of Hero, not for himself (as Claudio fears) but, rather, for Claudio. Claudio will get his Hero after all, and the marriage has the blessing of Hero's father, Leonato, to boot.

Claudio's rush to judgment works against him a second time, in an even more dramatic fashion. In fact, Claudio's behavior very nearly causes a tragedy. With the aid of Borachio, Don John orchestrates a little performance in which Claudio is led to believe that Hero is having an affair. Claudio witnesses a woman he thinks is Hero making love with Borachio at her balcony window. The whole scene has been arranged ahead of time, as we in the audience know: it is not Hero but Margaret, her serving-woman, whom Claudio spies in Borachio's embrace. Again, Claudio is prepared to think the worst, so he proceeds to attack Hero verbally at their wedding altar the next day by accusing her of lying about being a virgin and honorable. He angrily gives his intended bride back to her father:

59

There, Leonato, take her back again.
Give not this rotten orange to your friend;
She's but the sign and semblance of her honour.
Behold how like a maid she blushes here!
Oh, what authority and show of truth
Can cunning sin cover itself withal!
Comes not that blood as modest evidence
To witness simple virtue? Would you not swear,
All you that see her, that she were a maid,
By these exterior shows? But she is none:
She knows the heat of a luxurious bed.
Her blush is guiltiness, not modesty.

(4.1.30–41)

This scene, in which Claudio publicly humiliates both Hero and her father, is the most intense and emotionally violent scene in the play. Seeing his daughter's reputation destroyed, Leonato expresses a wish to die ("Hath no man's dagger here a point for me?" [109]). Like Claudio, Leonato is also willing to believe the false rumors about his daughter ("Would the two princes lie and Claudio lie?" [152]), and in his ranting he actually wishes her dead. Only through the intercession of Benedick and the Friar is Leonato calmed down enough to pause in his indictment of his daughter.

This segment of the story carries some eerie foreshadowing of *Othello*. Claudio seems to be obsessed with images of women's sexuality as threatening and volatile ("beauty is a witch"), and he is easily led into destructive fantasies ("she knows the heat of a luxurious bed"). His response when his faith is tested is to lash out violently. If not for the benign intervention of his friends (and Hero's incredibly forgiving nature), Claudio would doom himself to a life of guilt-ridden isolation.

Two key events occur in the story to return the play to its comic course. First, Constable Dogberry and his watchmen manage by good luck to discover and unravel the plot laid by Don John and Borachio. They also force the villains to confess that Claudio was set up and that Hero is completely innocent. Second, Leonato, Hero, and the Friar concoct a way to teach Claudio a lesson while getting him back together with Hero after all. They convince Claudio that Hero has died of shame, and after forcing him to perform public penance at her tomb, they get him to agree to marry Antonio's daughter in recompense. This fictive daughter is then unveiled as Hero herself, who is not dead after all ("She died, my lord, but whiles her slander lived" [5.4.65]). The play manages to use Don John as the villainous scapegoat, and his reported capture at the very end restores a sense of poetic justice to the story. Nonetheless, *Much Ado*, like *A Midsummer Night's Dream*, unleashes some disturbing and potentially tragic energies that its hasty resolution cannot entirely contain. Perhaps that is Shakespeare's point.

While the movement of the Claudio—Hero story provides the basic plot device which drives the play onwards, the relationship of Beatrice and Benedick provides its emotional and psychological center, and its depth. Beatrice and Benedick are among the most compelling and memorable characters in all of Shakespeare's comedies. They are smart, self-aware, realistic, and perceptive. Where Claudio is consumed with the appearance of things, Benedick (his counterpart) is quick to see through to the underlying truth. Benedick is convinced of Hero's innocence throughout, for example. Beatrice and Benedick are both good judges of character, shrewd observers of the people and events around them.

Beatrice and Benedick stand at the opposite end of the spectrum from Claudio and Hero. They are both too smart to buy into conventional wisdom, and they pay a price for that. So, their relationship is described by Leonato as "a kind of merry war" (1.1.57). The play gives us some hints that they have been romantically involved with one another in the past and that the results were not good. (See 2.1, especially lines 265–268.) They have both grown so proudly attached to their aloof status as single people that they have to be tricked by their friends into admitting their love for each other. Benedick neatly expresses his lofty expectations for a mate in the following terms: "but till all graces be in one woman, one woman shall not come in my grace" (2.3.29–31). Benedick's all-or-nothing standards are shared by Beatrice. When her uncle, Leonato, says to her that he hopes "to see [her] . . . one day fitted with a husband," her response is "Not till God make men of some other metal than earth" (2.1.53–56).

The process through which these two cynics are drawn together forms one of the most important movements in the plot of *Much Ado*. Their direct exchanges sometimes take place masked; so, they know they are talking to each other but pretend not to know they are. They are manipulated by their friends, who artfully arrange staged performances for the benefit of the eavesdropping protagonists. Only when each is let in on the secret of the other's feelings does either one of them openly admit to themselves that they do indeed feel something for the other. But clearly Beatrice and Benedick possess a mature self-awareness that Claudio and Hero lack. Beatrice and Benedick are able to see through social convention in order to develop a more authentic intimacy.

Branagh's Much Ado about Nothing *(1993)*

Kenneth Branagh's 1993 film of *Much Ado* is one of very few Shakespeare films to achieve both critical and popular success. Branagh's acting, in the role of Benedick, opposite Emma Thompson's strong and self-assured Beatrice, contributes greatly to the film. Denzel Washington and Keanu Reaves add box-office drawing power, and Michael Keaton as Dogberry brings an element of comic genius and outrageous charm. The film is set in a lush Italian villa, which adds an aura of earthy, summery sensuality to the film, an aura that enhances the already vibrant eroticism of the play itself.

One interesting formal element in Branagh's film is the use of a song ("Sigh no more, ladies, sigh no more" [61–76]) as a framing device and motif throughout the film. This song appears in Shakespeare's text in Act 2, Scene 3, but Branagh moves it to a more prominent position. As the film begins, the words to this song appear sequentially on an otherwise blank screen as they are read by Emma Thompson in voice-over. The first image we see is an unfinished watercolor painting of an Italian villa. The camera pans left to reveal the actual villa in the distance beyond the edge of the painting. The residents of Leonato's Messina are lolling about in the summer sun and enjoying a late afternoon picnic. As the camera continues its slow pan left, we finally come to rest on Beatrice (Thompson) sitting in a tree reading the song to the gathered audience. The lines of the song form an effective sound bridge that crosses from off-screen to on-screen space.

Much later in the film (in Act 5, Scene 2), Beatrice (Thompson) and Benedick (Branagh) engage in an animated conversation—one among several in the play. Beatrice has come to ask Benedick whether he has followed through on his promise to challenge Claudio to a duel. When she asks what has passed between them, Benedick replies, "Only foul words; and thereupon I will kiss you." But she turns it back on him: "Foul words is but foul wind, and foul wind is but foul breath, and foul breath is noisome; therefore I will depart unkissed" (5.2.48–52). In the scene, Branagh (as director) uses the window to frame the shot as well as the verdant Italian countryside in the background.

It's also important to pay attention to Branagh's use of two of the primary dramatic devices in the play: masks and eavesdropping. The masked ball presented in Act 2 contains numerous instances of willful as well as accidental misrecognition as the characters are all masked. Both Beatrice and Benedick are tricked by their friends, who intentionally stage conversations they want the protagonists to overhear.

Analysis and Interpretation: Much Ado about Nothing

1. To what extent is Branagh's film concerned with the nature of honesty in human relationships? What sorts of honesty does each of the major characters display during the course of the drama? What role does their self-awareness (or lack thereof) play in their attitude to honesty?

2. Some reviewers have commented that Branagh makes Claudio more sympathetic to audiences than does the original play. Do you agree? What changes has Branagh made in the script and in the presentation of the story that would support the view that he wants to present a more likable Claudio in his film?

3. Find an example of a scene where a character is masked or where one character is eavesdropping on a conversation. How does Branagh handle these scenes? What functions does the device of the mask or of overhearing serve in this film? What do characters learn or discover when they are hidden or disguised? How do their discoveries affect them?

4. Re-read the complete text of the song that appears in the play at 2.3.61–76. How do you explicate these lines? When Branagh uses them as a kind of epigraph to his film, what themes does it emphasize? Does the film support the statement that "men were deceivers ever"?

Twelfth Night; or, What You Will

The title *Twelfth Night* refers to the twelfth night of Christmas, celebrated in Shakespeare's time as The Feast of the Epiphany (January 6). The twelve days of Christmas were a time of celebration and revelry, which culminated in the carnival atmosphere of Twelfth Night itself. As in some of the other comedies, seasonal revelry offers an opportunity to turn authority or convention on its head and for fools to become philosophers and kings for a while.

This dramatic reversal is perhaps most evident in the stories of Feste and Malvolio. In *Twelfth Night*, Feste is a traveling minstrel-fool who entertains the locals with songs and wit. He takes part in a plot to undo Malvolio, the kill-joy steward of Lady Olivia's household and someone who is always enforcing quiet and decorum. Feste ends up pretending to be a priest while Malvolio is locked up in darkness and accused of being insane. Feste often seems to be the sanest, wisest person in the play, even though he is a homeless beggar. His role prefigures other wise fools, most notably the Fool in *King Lear*.

A related inversion of appearances takes place when Viola disguises herself as "Cesario"—a young man—in order to take cover in the world of Duke Orsino's court. Disguised as Cesario, Viola serves as Orsino's emissary. He/she pleads his (Orsino's) case to Olivia, who continues to rebuff his every advance. In the course of this plot, things get very confused: Olivia falls in love with Cesario/Viola, a woman she thinks is a man. Viola falls in love with Orsino even as he/she pretends to be Cesario. And Orsino, pining away melodramatically for Olivia, confides in and befriends Cesario without realizing that his young friend is actually a woman. The play presents a modern concept of gender as appearance and convention as it seeks to confuse and then unravel all the misdirected desires of its main characters. As in most of the comedies, the couples are sorted out into conventionally heterosexual couples by the end (thanks to the appearance of Viola's identical twin brother, Sebastian). At the same time, the homoerotic subtexts are strongly present, available to be either exploited or avoided in performance and film.

Nunn's Twelfth Night *(1996)*

Although several made-for-TV versions of *Twelfth Night* have been done (most recently, a 2003 modernized version directed by Tim Supple), Trevor Nunn's stylish 1996 interpretation remains the only feature film of the play that has been made to date. Shot on the rocky Cornwall coastline, Nunn's film is set in the early nineteenth century with uniforms and costumes that suggest a timeframe somewhere around the Napoleonic wars. Nunn's Feste, played by Ben Kingsley, functions as a chorus or narrator. His songs frame the beginning and end of the film, and Kingsley occasionally makes direct eye contact with the camera/viewer—even winking at us at the end of the film. His interpretation of Feste brings a note of melancholy existentialism to the film, for his languid songs evoke the passing of time and the coming of death. His repeated insistence that we should seize the day comes more from the resignation of old age than from the exuberance of youth.

In the realist medium of film, it's somewhat hard to believe that Viola (Imogen Stubbs) could be mistaken for a man. (It's worth remembering that Shakespeare's Viola would have been played by an adolescent male, hence Cesario would appear on stage as a young man pretending to be a woman pretending to be a man.) There are a few moments when characters flirt with same-sex kisses or embraces, but the film studiously, and perhaps fastidiously, avoids anything more than a close call among the gender-confused pairs.

Nonetheless, Nunn's actors manage to bring both humor and pathos to their roles as the film successfully finds a balance between the humor and the darker philosophical elements of the play.

The ending sequence of *Twelfth Night* shows both the establishment of the new society and the departure (or exile) of those characters that have no place in this new society. Nunn intercuts scenes from the wedding dance in lavish costumes with shots of individual characters departing the world of Olivia's household. One by one, Antonio, Malvolio, and Maria depart, Malvolio rather sadly with suitcase and umbrella in hand. He has vowed revenge and leaves to escape the indignities he has experienced at the hands of Maria and Sir Toby. Maria leaves in disgrace and presumably at Olivia's request because of her role in the sinister plot to abuse Malvolio. Antonio leaves simply because there's no place for him in the new order: His Sebastian is now linked to Olivia. The film's closing sequence shows how the happy world of the two couples establishes itself by banishing certain others who no longer have a place in it. Finally, Feste himself, who has served as our narrator and whose song (" For the rain it raineth every day" [5.1.389–408]) accompanies the film's ending sequence, gives us a wink, shoulders his satchel and lute, and walks off down the hill and out of the frame.

Analysis and Interpretation: Twelfth Night

1. What is the relationship between friendship and romantic love in Nunn's film? Do the characters discover that friendship is the best basis for romantic and sexual love? How do the two main plots/couples compare and contrast on this issue? Is Orsino's attraction to Cesario/Viola different from Olivia's attraction to Cesario/Sebastian? Why or why not?

2. Explicate the songs sung by Feste at the beginning and end of the film. How does each relate to the major themes of the play? What role does Kingsley's Feste play in the world of *Twelfth Night?* What is he doing there, and how does he influence people or events?

3. The Malvolio subplot involves manipulation and deceit, much like Don John's treatment of Claudio in *Much Ado.* Who tricks

Malvolio and why? To what degree does their plot succeed? Are we supposed to feel that Malvolio gets his due? Why or why not? What kind of justice (if any) is served by what happens to him?

4. How do the setting and the scenery of the film contribute to its thematic feel and atmosphere? What effect does the rocky coastline have on certain scenes? How else is setting and *mise-en-scene* used to create an emotional effect?

CHAPTER 3

The Histories

As we move from the comedies to the histories, we come upon a very different world. Unlike the comedies, whose sources derive from literary tradition, folklore, and popular culture, the history plays are based on real events and historical figures. More precisely, the history plays are based on historical sources, primarily Holinshed's *Chronicles* and Hall's *Union of the Two Noble and Illustre* [sic] *Families of Lancaster and York*. It is important to remember that Shakespeare was a dramatist not a historian, but he found in English history a rich vein of dramatic conflict and dynastic struggle to mine and refine for the stage.

In the history plays, we enter the arena of politics, conflict, violence, and warfare. The themes that emerge in the histories concern the nature of kingship and political authority, the rules of succession and the right to the crown, the shaping of the political state, and the importance of social order and hierarchy. While there are notable moments of humor and romance in the history plays, they are often darker and more serious in tone, as one might expect, than are such moments in the comedies.

The Importance of History to Elizabethan England

Shakespeare's history plays form two groups of four plays (or tetralogies). Together, they cover the period known as the Wars of the Roses, which lasted from about 1398 until 1485. (See the end of this chapter for a chronology of the history plays.) Two other historical plays, *King John* and *Henry VIII*, are not directly a part of this sequence since King John reigned at a much earlier time (1199–1216) and Henry VIII at a slightly later period (1509–1547). It's important to remember that Shakespeare was writing about events relatively far in the past even in his own day though his two history tetralogies do conclude with the accession to the throne of Elizabeth I's grandfather, Henry VII. The Wars of the Roses ended with the battle of Bosworth Field in 1485—more than a century before Shakespeare's history plays were written in the 1590s. This historical gap is roughly equal to an American today writing a series of plays about the period from the War of 1812 to the end of World War I in 1918. By the time Shakespeare wrote about the Wars of the Roses, those historical events had already been at least partially transformed into myth and legend. Since then and with a measure of irony, Shakespeare's plays themselves have come to color our view of the people and events of those times—they have themselves become mythic.

Why would audiences in Shakespeare's day have been interested in history as a subject for drama? We know that the English history play enjoyed a period of great popularity in the 1590s, and that Shakespeare was one of several authors (albeit the greatest) developing major sequences of history plays for the theaters of the day. In part, this popularity was related to the rising status of England in the political world of the late sixteenth century. With its defeat of the Spanish Armada in 1588, England began to assume an unprecedented position of ascendancy on the world political stage. The nation entered a period of economic confidence and national pride. One outgrowth of this sense of importance was a desire to explore the historical developments and events that had brought England to its position of prominence and relative stability.

In part, also, political conflict and religious turmoil were roiling beneath the surface, so there was a significant degree of propaganda to a literary genre whose purpose was to justify and naturalize the existing Elizabethan political order. Catholic loyalists continued to resist the tide of the Protestant Reformation at the end of the sixteenth century. Queen Elizabeth herself had no direct heir and, so, left the question of succession in doubt. Indeed, fewer than 40 years after her death the nation would again slide into civil war, so there was something crucial at stake in writing (and, more significantly, rewriting) history so as to justify and celebrate the existing regime.

Many in Shakespeare's audiences would be drawn to take lessons and parallels for their own times from the stories played out on the stage before them. To that extent, the Wars of the Roses and the history plays served as cautionary tales for a nation enjoying a period of prosperity and stability that many feared could not last forever. The historical moment was filled with ambivalence and possibility, so Shakespeare and his fellow playwrights along with their audiences looked with particular interest at the recent past in an effort to understand their present.

Interpreting the Past

When Shakespeare and his contemporaries looked back at the history of the previous two centuries, they had a couple of frameworks by means of which to interpret the past. The first of these was what might be called the medieval or providential view of history. This view held that people and events were players in a divine plan on a grand scale. The Wars of the Roses, according to this view, were part of a divine process of punishment and restitution brought about by the arrogance and selfishness of the English people. In general, the "official" historians and chroniclers of the day subscribed to this view; their rhetorical goal was to legitimize the Tudor dynasty and to glorify Queen Elizabeth and her government. The second framework was a more modern one, and some of Shakespeare's audiences would likely have adopted such a perspective. For them, history would have seemed more human than divine. For them, history would have been a process driven by rhetoric, power, contingency, and luck more than by providence. In the history plays, we often see these two views portrayed simultaneously (Shakespeare is nothing if not complex), and the dramatic tension in the plays themselves often derives from an inability to choose between them. History is reworked by Shakespeare to make it interesting as theater, and this reworking usually means deliberately creating a narrative that can be read in multiple ways.

This ambiguity or multiplicity is further complicated when we shift our attention to modern films based on these Shakespearean history plays. Shakespeare was already re-interpreting the events of the past through his own experience and social context. A modern film adds a third layer: that of the times in which the film itself was made. One of the two films of *Richard III* discussed in this chapter, for example, makes historical layering explicit. Richard Loncraine's 1995 film uses Nazi-era uniforms and imagery to link King Richard III to Hitler and the fascist movements of the 1930s. Obviously, Shakespeare could not have anticipated the horrors of the twentieth century, but Loncraine's use of visual iconography from the Nazi era suggests ways in which King Richard's political theater and rhetoric may be seen as a precursor to more familiar and more recent power politics and the manipulations of mass media. Even when filmmakers are less explicit than Loncraine was in doing so, their films inevitably project their own era's struggles and concerns onto the dramatic conflicts in the plays.

Analysis and Interpretation: Shakespeare's History Plays

1. How do the history plays represent history as a literary and dramatic subject? What types of events do the history plays chronicle?

2. Who are the primary characters in the history plays? What qualities and values do they embody? How are we meant to respond to their actions?

3. What dramatic conflicts drive the actions of the history plays? What seems to be at stake in particular characters' actions and words?

4. What evidence in the plays suggests or supports a view of history as the enactment of providence or God's plan? What evidence undercuts or counters this view?

5. It's often said that the purpose of studying history is to avoid repeating the mistakes of the past. What evidence suggests a didactic or pedagogical purpose in the history plays?

6. How are contemporary ideas about history like or unlike the ideas presented in the plays? Has our theory of history changed? If so, how? Do you see any modern parallels to events or characters in

the histories? What events or time periods have been the subject of modern history plays (or films)?

The Histories on Film

The two history plays that have been the primary focus of modern filmmakers contrast with each other in a revealing way. *Henry V* stands as a triumphant, heroic conclusion to the sequence of four plays that begins with *Richard II* and proceeds through the first and second parts of *Henry IV*. After more than a decade of civil war (in the Wars of the Roses), Henry's astonishing military victory over the French at Agincourt in 1415 cemented his authority and ended the civil strife—at least for a short time. To a significant degree, Henry is portrayed as a model king, and certainly Shakespeare's most heroic monarch. As radical contrast, Richard III (the "bloody dog" as Richmond calls him at the end of the play) is his most villainous by a country mile. The plot of *Richard III* traces Richard of Gloucester's murderous rise to power and the throne at the expense of all who dare to stand in his way. As clearly as Henry V is king-as-hero, Richard III is king-as-villain. Where Henry V concludes one tetralogy on a high note, Richard III concludes the other with a rapid decline into violence and chaos.

Perhaps it is these extremes, as well as the two plays' clear focus on a single central character, that have made these dramas popular for adapting to the screen. *Richard III* was filmed as early as 1911 in England (by Frank Benson) and 1912 in the United States (by André Calmettes and James Keane). However, it is Laurence Olivier's 1955 version that stood for four decades as the definitive interpretation. With the exception of a Swiss production in 1986 directed by Raoul Ruiz, another film version of *Richard III* was not attempted until 1995. In that year, Ian McKellen and Richard Loncraine made a visually striking version set in a fascist 1930s context. *Henry V* has been the subject of two major feature films: Laurence Olivier's 1944 production, usually seen as a patriotic work of wartime propaganda, and Kenneth Branagh's darker, more ambiguous 1989 version.

Richard III

Representing both the end of the story of the Wars of the Roses and the end of Shakespeare's first English history tetralogy (the so-called "minor" tetralogy), *Richard III* raises important questions relevant to all of the history plays. As one of the most ruthless, Machiavellian figures in any of the plays, Richard, Duke of Gloucester (later King Richard III) can be seen as both a type and as an individual. As he manipulates and murders his way to the throne, we wonder to what extent we are watching a modern psychological drama and to what degree a medieval allegory. Is Richard an allegorical character, a figure whose evil is so complete and predetermined that his eventual death cleanses the whole national landscape and, so, clears the way for a fresh start in the person of Henry VII (Henry Tudor)? Is his physical deformity an outward symbol of some curse or predestined role? Or is he a modern villain instead, a master of political rhetoric and theater, whose major mistakes can be read as miscalculation rather than divine retribution?

Richard III: *Olivier (1955) and Branagh (1995)*

Because Shakespeare gives plausible weight to either (or *both*) of these readings, actors and filmmakers have had considerable room to develop their own portrayals of Richard and his story. As viewers of these films, we are granted an unusual kind of intimacy with our villain. In their performances, both Olivier and McKellen use direct eye-contact with the camera in order to draw us into their world and to give us glimpses into Richard's thoughts and motives that none of the other characters in the drama have or could have. Under both Olivier's and Loncraine's direction, the camera often follows Richard around during key soliloquies, and we are often visually aligned with his point of view during the action in important sequences. Olivier makes brilliant use of a set in which we frequently stand with Richard at a window or on a balcony, so we overlook the main action as we overhear Richard's musings and his commentary on what is taking place.

In Shakespeare's play, the famous opening soliloquy (1.1.1–41) with its inspired pun ("Now is the winter of our discontent / Made glorious summer by this son [sun?] of York") quickly establishes Richard's character as it builds the audience's sense of intimacy with him, however unpleasant he may be. Explaining that he is "not shaped for sportive tricks," our Richard vows instead "to prove a villain." "I am subtle, false, and treacherous," he tells us as he reveals—before we are even 40 lines into the play—his plan to set his brothers Clarence and King Edward IV against one another. Following quickly on the heels of this revelation, the second major scene of the play contains what has to stand as one of the most improbable courtship scenes in all of Shakespeare. Having killed her husband (Prince Edward, son of King Henry VI), Richard now woos Lady Anne as they stand over the corpse of Henry VI, her late father-in-law. "He that bereft thee, lady, of thy husband / Did it to help thee to a better husband" (1.2.141–142). "'Twas thy heavenly face that set me on," Richard asserts. He offers to let her kill him in revenge; he offers to kill himself if she wishes; he has placed an engagement ring on her finger by the end of the scene. As she and the pallbearers exit carrying the body of Henry VI, we are again alone with Richard: "Was ever woman in this humor wooed?" he asks (1.2.230). Dumbfounded, we are inclined to answer aloud: "No. You're right. Never."

In truth, the character of Richard does not develop or unfold so much as explode onto the stage in Shakespeare's play. Hovering ominously in the background (and sometimes in the foreground) of the previous plays, he now takes center stage as a fully formed villain. Few of Shakespeare's plays open as quickly, starkly, or brilliantly as *Richard III*. How do filmmakers work to achieve similar effects in their opening moments?

Olivier opens his 1955 film with a vibrant and colorful coronation scene. (The film's use of the VistaVision film format with its finer clarity made the scene even more striking visually.) As the new king, Edward IV, is crowned, Richard looks on from the wings. As soon as the royal procession moves off down the street, the camera turns back towards Richard. A heavy door opens slowly (apparently on its own) to show the now-empty throne room, and we follow the

74

camera's movement in to where Richard (now alone) addresses his opening lines, a soliloquy, directly to us. Sustained, direct eye-contact links us with him, and for most of the rest of the film our point of view aligns closely with his.

Richard Loncraine and Ian McKellen (in the 1995 version) insert their own sequence of events prior to the coronation scene. King Henry VI and his son, Prince Edward, are at their battle headquarters in Tewkesbury. (The military uniforms and equipment situate the scene somewhere in the late 1930s.) A message comes over the tickertape: "Richard Gloucester is at hand. He holds his course towards Tewkesbury." As Edward sits down to his dinner, a heavy vibration begins to rattle his wine glass. A tank crashes through the wall into the room and armed men in gas masks rush at him and kill him with machine-gun fire and a final bullet between the eyes. We cut to King Henry saying what he knows will be his final prayers. Still wearing a gas mask, Richard's face is hidden, but we immediately recognize his pronounced limp and useless left arm. His loud breathing in the mask cannot help but remind us of another legendary film villain—Darth Vader. Killing the king with a single shot to the back of the head, Richard (McKellen) pulls off his mask as the film's title marches across the screen in large, blood-red capital letters.

We move next to the sumptuous coronation of the new king, Edward IV. After some music and dancing, Richard addresses the assembled celebrants from the microphone on the dance-band's dais. As he speaks the opening lines of his famous soliloquy, the camera closes in on his mouth (suggesting, perhaps, the power of his rhetoric). Suddenly, the tone and the scene shift. We find ourselves at a urinal in the men's room. The second half of Richard's opening speech is spoken in deeply sarcastic tones as he empties his bladder. As he washes his hands, he continues to speak, evidently addressing his own reflection in the mirror. Suddenly, he catches our eye (the camera's) in the mirror. Startlingly, he turns to speak directly to us: "and therefore, since I cannot prove a lover / . . . I am determined to prove a villain." Much as Olivier's camera draws us into a forced intimacy with his Richard, so too does Loncraine's restroom sequence place us squarely and immediately into a private space that

75

only we and Richard share. Both Olivier's and Loncraine's opening sequences can be seen as effective cinematic adaptations of the dramatic soliloquy used so effectively by Shakespeare. Both crisply characterize Richard and, at the same time, establish an intimate relationship between the arch-villain and his audience.

Richard is in fact both an actor and a director as the story unfolds. He is explicit about the role acting plays in his self-created political theater. In a scene from one of Shakespeare's earlier history plays, *Henry VI, Part 3* (incorporated by Olivier into Richard's opening soliloquy in *Richard III*), Richard avers, "Why, I can smile, and murder whiles I smile, / . . . and wet my cheeks with artificial tears, / And frame my face to all occasions" (3.2.182–185). Because both films grant us an inside view of Richard, we are able to interpret—as most of the characters in the drama are not—when he is acting. We recognize, as they cannot, the distance between what he presents as a façade and what he is actually thinking and doing. The effect is to lend a deep, persistent irony to the story as we are privileged with the heavy and disconcerting knowledge that Richard's motivations are always sinister and self-serving.

Richard directs scenes as well as acting in them: One key example of this combined role is the breathtakingly manipulative scene in which the townspeople of London come to him and ask him to be king. He presents himself as the devout worshipper engaged in his daily devotions with two clergymen at his side. He resists the people's invitation to become king, for he knows that the more he appears reluctant the more they will pursue him. With the help of his confidant Buckingham, Richard stages the entire event as theater. His efforts are successful. To the acclaim of the Mayor and citizens of London, Richard is hailed as the next King of England.

The conclusion of the story unfolds quickly and almost inevitably. In his ruthless rise to power, Richard alienates all of his followers, even the loyal Buckingham. They flock to Richmond's side and help to defeat Richard in battle at Bosworth Field as Richard famously and vainly calls out: "A horse! A horse! My kingdom for a horse!" (5.4.13). Richard's ill-won gains prove to be of less worth than a *single* horse, and his death returns a sense of stability and justice to the land: "the bloody dog is dead" says his rival, Richmond (5.5.2). The end of *Richard III* coincided with the end of a century of war and dynastic conflict and with the beginning of the Tudor dynasty, a family of rulers who, of course, climaxed with Queen Elizabeth (Richmond/Henry VII's granddaughter), who ruled England for most of Shakespeare's life.

Despite the sense of poetic justice we are expected to share at Richard's demise, both film versions of *Richard III* succeed in leaving us haunted by a series of troubling questions. Richard has effectively demonstrated that politics and kingship are matters of performance. His world is a strikingly modern one in which image is everything, a world in which the people will believe what they are led to believe. Olivier's film creates the lingering impression that perhaps all politics is about appearance rather than reality. His Richard remains a compelling figure even in his excesses. Loncraine's film brings these issues even more explicitly into focus; his modern setting connects Richard to fascism and suggests that other forms of the cult of personality may be equally successful, especially during times of crisis. The play's resolution is, on one level, meant to signal a return of peace and stability, but both films leave viewers with a suspicion that Richard is a Machiavellian, even Hitlerian, prototype, a prototype of which we have not seen the last.

Analysis and Interpretation: Richard III

1. Olivier's film adds a number of lines from *Henry VI, Part 3* to Richard's opening soliloquy. (See the end of Act 3, Scene 2 of that play.) What was Olivier's purpose in doing so? What do these additional lines reveal about Richard?

2. Loncraine and McKellen's screenplay cuts about two-thirds of the lines from Shakespeare's play. How do you think they made decisions about what to cut and what to keep? Does such a radical editing of the play work?

3. Why do you think Olivier and Loncraine chose *Richard III* to remake as a film? What about the play makes it attractive for reworking in cinematic terms? Why would a film based on this history be attractive to modern audiences?

4. Both Olivier and Loncraine use a variety of film techniques to build the audience's relationship with the main character. Besides direct eye-contact with the camera, what other techniques do their films use to create an intimate relationship with Richard? Does Richard become a more "sympathetic" character as a result? Why or why not?

5. Olivier's version of the play was filmed almost entirely indoors on small-scale sets at Shepperton Studios in England. (The exception was the battle scenes late in the drama, which were filmed outdoors in Spain.) How does Olivier use this enclosed set to create mood and tension? Make note of the points at which doorways and windows are used to frame characters or scenes. How do these visual boundaries work to define the story space of the film?

6. Loncraine makes a pointed and bold decision to set his film in the 1930s. While the language is still taken directly from Shakespeare's text, the art direction and visual elements create a world that few viewers would recognize as "traditional Shakespeare." What is the effect of this radical chronological shift?

7. Both Olivier and Loncraine use *Richard III* to present a view of politics as stagecraft or illusion. Why does Richard fail if he is so good at "acting" like a king? Is there evidence in either film that politics is something other than manipulation or theater? If not through the power of rhetoric and political theater, how would the "ideal" king rule?

8. The crown is used repeatedly as a symbol in Olivier's film. How does this icon function to suggest some kind of ideal of kingship? What values or power is the crown meant to signify?

Henry V

The opening scenes of *Henry V* raise important questions about the right of one ruler or country to invade another. In the first major action of the play, King Henry consults with his bishops and lords about the legal and moral justifications for invading France in order to assert his claim to the French throne. While the bishops assure

Henry that he has both a legal and a moral right to wage war on France for the purpose of claiming the crown, we know from the play's very first scene that their motivations are in fact self-serving. All of the legal and theological justifications for Henry's war on France are suspect, for they constitute a diversionary tactic the Archbishop of Canterbury and the Bishop of Ely devise to keep King Henry distracted from a pending parliamentary bill that would strip the church of much of its lands and wealth.

Nonetheless, Henry's French campaign ends in his success, both in war and in love. Outnumbered significantly, his army wins a resounding, improbable, but historically accurate victory on the battlefield at Agincourt. To cement the rise to power of the new Anglo-French monarchy, by the end of the play Henry has succeeded in winning the hand of Katharine (de Valois), daughter of France's king, Charles VI. The play ends as preparations are being made for their wedding. The closing lines of the play, spoken by the Chorus, describe King Henry as "this star of England" (Epilogue 6). *Henry V* ends at the very pinnacle of success, but the Chorus reminds us the triumph will be short-lived. Upon Henry's death, his son is "in infant bands crowned King" (Epilogue 9), and Shakespeare's audience would have known of the return of war and the loss of France under Henry VI that was so soon to come.

If Richard III serves as the model villain in Shakespeare's histories, Henry V stands in marked contrast as the model King. The preceding plays, the first and second parts of *Henry IV*, have chronicled his youth as Prince Hal, a youth notoriously misspent drinking and clubbing and womanizing in the company of Falstaff. Yet, it turns out that his youthful excesses have humanized him and made him a more well-rounded, compassionate ruler as he succeeds to the throne as Henry V. He is able to understand the common people. His speeches to his troops on the eve of the battle at Agincourt amply demonstrate this ability. While "the courses of his youth promised it not" (1.1.25), Henry has matured and grown into the role of king in a remarkable way:

> The breath no sooner left his father's body,
> But that his wildness, mortified in him,

79

Seem'd to die too; yea, at that very moment
Consideration, like an angel, came
And whipp'd the offending Adam out of him,
Leaving his body as a paradise,
To envelop and contain celestial spirits.
(1.1.26–32)

In this sudden transformation, Hal's wildness is remade by
"consideration" (that is, reflection or meditation). The star of
England emerges from the pubs and brothels of his wild and
misspent youth a permanently changed man.

Henry V: *Olivier (1944) and Branagh (1989)*

Two feature films present quite different visions of Henry as king.
Laurence Olivier's 1944 film works hard to present a patriotic,
gleaming image of the king. To do so, Olivier simply leaves out some
of the scenes that show a darker side to the man. He chooses instead
to create a film that presents the star of England in colorful,
unmediated glory. Kenneth Branagh's 1989 film offers a powerful
and dark contrast to Olivier's earlier take on England's most famous
king. We are made to see the violent and extreme side of political
authority, and the battle scenes are dark, muddy, and realistic.
Branagh's Henry must execute friends and threaten disproportionate,
vengeful, violent retaliation on the people of the town of Harfleur.
Branagh's Henry undoubtedly knows too some of what Richard III
knows about politics as theater. His Henry seems, at least on the
surface, much more in keeping with a skeptical modern view of
political authority.

The visual styles of the two films also stand in marked contrast to
one another. On board ship bound for France, Olivier as Henry V is
colorfully depicted against a sunny background. Even patriotic
overtones are apparent in the King's posture. Branagh as King Henry
spends some of his time on a muddy battlefield following his
astonishing victory at Agincourt. His weariness *even in victory* and the
bloody corpses stacked in the wagon where he stands to speak paint a
very different picture of war than what we see in the Olivier film.

80

As we noted in Chapter 1, Olivier's film begins with a historical re-enactment of the Globe theater and the play as it might have been performed in 1600. His sets are two-dimensional, painterly, and evoke a medieval Book of Hours. The film has the look of a puppet show rather than a realistic military drama. Branagh also employs an elaborate framing device and the figure of the Chorus to mediate between us and the events of the film, but its look and style are more gritty and realistic. Is Shakespeare's Henry the glorious hero we see in Olivier's film? Or is he the dark and brooding figure of Branagh's re-visioning? As usual, Shakespeare provides ample textual support for both views. The subtlety of *Henry V* is that we have to see the central figure as both hero *and* Machiavellian manipulator. The resulting vision of kingship as power is remarkably ambivalent and contemporary. These qualities are certainly a part of the reason the play works so successfully on-screen for audiences today.

Analysis and Interpretation: Henry V

1. How does Olivier use the figure of the Chorus and the Globe's stage to frame the events of his film? What is the function of the Chorus in the film?

2. Branagh uses the Prologue and the Chorus to call our attention to the fact that we are watching a film, that is to say a constructed visual representation. What effect does this device have on our response to the events?

3. Make a list of important scenes from the play not included in Olivier's film. How many of these scenes are included in Branagh's version of the film? How do these scenes change the picture of Henry V that we see?

4. The Criterion DVD version of the Olivier *Henry V* includes a series of images taken from a medieval Book of Hours. Explore these images and think about their use as a model for the style of Olivier's film. The use of a two-dimensional painterly style is important in several scenes in the film. Which scenes most evidently rely on this style? What contrasting styles are used in other scenes? Is there a pattern to the way contrasting visual styles are used in the film?

5. How does Branagh's Chorus work to remind viewers of the artificiality of film as a medium? Does the Chorus's appearance on the battlefield affect your relationship to the events of the film? How? Why would Branagh want to use the Chorus in this manner?

6. Olivier's *Henry V* has been criticized as a piece of wartime propaganda. Do you agree with this criticism? What evidence from the film complicates or challenges this view?

7. Is Branagh's *Henry V*, as some viewers have suggested, more realistic or critical in its depiction of the king and his power? In what ways does the film present King Henry as myth or hero? In what ways does it present him "realistically"? Can it do both? How?

A Chronology of Shakespeare's History Plays

The "Major" Tetralogy

(Textual and historical evidence suggests these four plays were written later than the plays in the "minor" tetralogy even though they deal with earlier historical events.)

Play	Date Written	Dates and Events Covered
Richard II	1595	(1398–1399) Struggle between King Richard II and Henry Bolingbroke (later King Henry IV); deposition and murder of Richard II
Henry IV, Pt 1	1596–1597	(1402–1403) Uprisings in Scotland and Wales; Battle of Shrewsbury, at which Prince Hal kills Harry Percy (Hotspur)
Henry IV, Pt 2	1597	(1403–1413) From the aftermath of the Battle of Shrewsbury to the death of King Henry IV
Henry V	1599	(1415) Henry V's campaign in France; siege of Harfleur, military victory over French at Agincourt; plans for marriage to Katharine (de Valois) to cement link to French crown

The "Minor" Tetralogy

(Textual and historical evidence suggests these four plays were written earlier than the plays in the "major" tetralogy even though they deal with later historical events.)

Play	Date Written	Dates and Events Covered
Henry VI, Pt. 1	c. 1589–1592	(1422–1453) From the funeral of Henry V to the death of John Talbot, Earl of Shrewsbury. Henry accepts Margaret of Anjou as his queen.
Henry VI, Pt. 2	c. 1589–1592	(1445–1455) Marriage of Henry and Margaret; loss of French lands; up to first battle of St Albans
Henry VI, Pt. 3	c. 1589–1592	(1460–1471) The military phase of the Wars; from the aftermath of the first battle of St Albans to the defeat of Queen Margaret at Tewksbury.
Richard III	c. 1591–1594	(1471–1485) Death of King Edward IV; Richard Gloucester's rise to the Protectorship and his ruthless rise to the throne; Richmond's defeat of Richard at the battle of Bosworth Field; coronation as King Henry VII (the first Tudor king).

CHAPTER 4

The Tragedies

The DVD version of Kenneth Branagh's *Hamlet* (1996) includes a short special feature on the making of the film. In it, Robin Williams and Billy Crystal (each of whom has a small part in the film) imagine William Shakespeare trying to pitch *Hamlet* to a present-day film-industry executive. Playing the part of a cynical studio executive, Robin Williams says: "We're really excited. The whole first half is *just great*. Can we lose the ghost? It's just a lot of negativity. And that whole death thing—we'd like it at the end if *he* lives." And as executive producer, Billy Crystal says to Shakespeare: "Sorry, Bill. We're crazy about you here, we are; the hair, the beard, the whole thing. But it's just *too much of a downer*. Isn't there anything for Jim Carrey to do in this?" With their characteristic on-target wit, Williams and Crystal point to the difficulties inherent in filming Shakespearean tragedy for a modern audience. Such an audience often wants entertainment and escape, not *tragedy*; so filmmakers have to find ways to re-imagine tragedy in the visual medium of film for an audience who may well not be familiar with the plots of Shakespeare's great tragedies.

Fortunately for us, filmmakers have been both prolific and inventive in their approaches to the tragedies. The tragedies have been produced on film by some of our greatest directors and actors in a variety of different ways. From Laurence Olivier's black-and-white 1948 psychological exploration of *Hamlet* to Baz Luhrmann's edgy, postmodern re-interpretation of *Romeo and Juliet* in 1996, filmed versions of the tragedies offer a wider and more ambitious range of film texts to be explored than films of drama in any other genre. This chapter focuses on a broad range of Shakespeare's tragedies in order to bring out the remarkable achievement they represent as a totality:

So, we look (in chronological order of original creation) at *Titus Andronicus*, *Romeo and Juliet*, *Hamlet*, *Othello*, *King Lear*, and *Macbeth*.

Tragic Form and Structure

What makes a tragedy tragic? How are tragedies supposed to make us feel? What's the difference between a story that is simply "a downer," as Billy Crystal's imaginary film producer might say, and one that is "tragic" in a Shakespearean sense? Shakespeare himself never wrote any criticism or theory which would help us to understand his ideas about tragic drama and its function, so we have to look elsewhere. As it turns out, a large body of critical work has been devoted to tragedy, extending as far back as classical antiquity and the age of the great Greek tragedians: Aeschylus, Sophocles, and Euripides.

For the Greeks, at least as we understand them through Aristotle's *Poetics*, tragic drama served important social functions. For them, tragedy was not just about death and violence, nor was it supposed to be sentimental or maudlin. Instead, tragedy involved what Aristotle called *katharsis*, the process of purging emotions by arousing them. Specifically, Aristotle argued that tragedy works by purging audiences of the emotions of pity and fear by means of katharsis. If tragic characters are good people who suffer by chance or accident, we will feel pity for them because of their bad luck, but we will *also* feel that their downfall was profoundly unjust. By contrast, if the tragic characters are simply evil, we will probably feel that justice is served by their downfall and we won't feel much empathy for them. For katharsis to do its work on us, we need to feel both emotions at once. The tragic characters need to be good enough that we feel a sense of loss or pity at their ill luck, yet morally weak enough so that we also feel that, to a degree, they got what they deserved.

The lasting appeal of Shakespeare's tragedies on film suggests that his characters continue to offer this kind of subtle emotional and moral complexity for a modern audience. The great tragic figures such as Hamlet still work for us because we can see enough of ourselves in them that we do feel connected because we are like them in some important respects. Yet, they are also responsible for or complicit in their own downfall, so we understand their ends as at least partially deserved.

Comedy, as we saw in Chapter 2, generally progresses from one social order to another during the course of the play. Typically, a new society forms around the main characters at the end. By contrast, tragedy often disrupts the social order and leaves it fragmented at the end of the drama. Tragic characters raise questions that undermine our faith in there being a "natural" order to life; they set in motion powerful disruptive forces that tear society apart. Comic endings reassure audiences that the fabric of life has been repaired and restored, and that the central conflicts explored in the main action of the play have been resolved. By contrast, tragedy is much more about conflict, so tragic plots leave audiences feeling deeply disturbed and uncertain. Tragedies often end with the death or exile of their main characters, but, even in death, the tragic heroes usually leave in their wake unresolved concerns—in the audience as well as among the remaining characters on stage—about the spiritual and political health of the world they inhabited *as well as the audience's world.*

Where comedy involves, in Northrop Frye's view, the mythos of spring (a time of rebirth and renewal), tragedy involved the mythos of autumn (a more philosophical season of decline and fall). For Frye, as for Aristotle, tragedy focuses on a central character who is somewhat elevated above the "average" members of his or her society but is someone who remains below the level of a god. Using an elegant metaphor, Frye writes, "tragic heroes are so much the highest points in their human landscape that they seem the inevitable conductors of the power about them, great trees more likely to be struck by lightning than a clump of grass" is (207).

At the same time, however, it is important that tragic characters also have a human side that allows audiences to identify with them. Unlike gods or the characters of myth or epic, tragic heroes are subject to the same laws of nature and causality as we are. They are not magical or superhuman; they cannot escape the consequences of their own actions. As Frye puts it, "However thickly strewn a tragedy may be with ghosts, portents, witches, or oracles, we know that the tragic hero cannot simply rub a lamp and summon a genie to get him out of his trouble" (207).

Many of Shakespeare's tragic characters do fit Frye's model. Think of Othello, for example. Once he begins to follow the insidious seed of jealousy planted in his mind by Iago, he seems unable to retard its growth. He becomes caught up in a vortex of violence he himself has unleashed. Macbeth, too, fits Frye's model. Having started the downward momentum of tragedy with the murder of Duncan, he cannot stop its murderous course until he himself becomes a victim. King Lear begins by rashly dividing up his kingdom and divesting himself of his authority even as he tries to remain important in his country's affairs. The consequences of his actions at the beginning of the play are the death of his beloved daughter, Cordelia, and the ruin of the kingdom at the end. Even Hamlet, perhaps the most complex tragic hero in Shakespeare, is overwhelmed with the secret knowledge (given him by his father's ghost) that his father has been murdered by his uncle, Claudius. That knowledge eats away at Hamlet's sanity and causes him to seek vengeance against Claudius even as Claudius plots to kill him. The result? The death of the innocent Ophelia (whom Hamlet once loved) and the loss of the kingdom to an invader, Fortinbras. Frye offers an especially useful formulation of the predicament in which the tragic hero finds himself: "The tragic hero is very great as compared with us, but there is something else, something on the side of him opposite the audience, compared to which he is small. This something else may be called God, gods, fate, accident, fortune, necessity, circumstance, or any combination of these, but whatever it is the tragic hero is our mediator with it" (207).

As this process works itself out through the tragic drama, the plot works towards some kind of recognition, awareness, or truth. Aristotle described this tragic recognition as "a change from ignorance to knowledge" and Frye called it an "epiphany of law, of that which is and must be" (208). Frye's view is that, for Shakespeare, this law is connected to science in the early-modern period and its emerging view of nature: "The tragic process in Shakespeare is natural in the sense that it simply happens, whatever its cause, explanation, or relationships. Characters may grope about for conceptions of gods that kill us for their sport, or for a divinity that shapes our ends, but the action of tragedy will not abide our questions" (208).

Shakespearean tragedy maintains a delicate balance between fatalism and a sense of morality. As much as we might feel that a particular character is simply acting according to fate, we also feel—we *need* to feel—at the same time that he or she is making choices or taking actions that do shape the outcome. The plays would not be especially moving or, indeed, interesting if we simply felt that the characters were victims of fate. Conversely, we also *need* to feel that the tragic characters are not simply being punished for breaking some kind of moral code. Macbeth may be a murderer, but his story is not simply about revenge or poetic justice. His story is as much about wayward ambition, something with which any audience could connect. Shakespeare usually surrounds his tragic characters with others who interpret, comment on, and analyze what is happening, but somehow we always know that none of these interpretations satisfies, none quite gives us the whole story. Shakespeare's tragedies are different from the more-fatalistic classical Greek dramas, and they are also a step or two away from modern existentialism (with its underlying sense that life is absurd). Multiple interpretations are almost always presented to the audience of a Shakespeare tragedy, and this multiplicity lends the tragedies a great deal of depth and complexity as subjects for films.

Analysis and Interpretation: Shakespearean Tragedy

1. Look at the main character in one of the tragedies. How does this character compare to other characters in the play? What are his or her attributes, qualities, or talents? What elevates this character above social norms?

2. What forces or events in the play seem to have power over (or be greater than) the main character? What drives or motivates the main character? Are there any supernatural or nonhuman forces in the play (ghosts, gods, prophets, fate)? On what authority do these nonhuman characters speak? How do they influence the thoughts and actions of the main character?

3. Look for characters in the play who comment on the action. (For example, Polonius, who interprets Hamlet's behavior as evidence that he is lovesick for Ophelia, or Kent, who critiques Lear's behavior at every turn.) What interpretation do these characters offer? How convincing are their comments or analyses?

4. Find the key moments of recognition and/or reversal in the plot. At what point does the direction of the plot shift or change? Why? Is there a clearly identifiable moment of truth or recognition? What is recognized? By whom?

5. Instead of looking for a single tragic flaw in the main character, list as many possible traits or motivations that might *possibly* account for that character's actions or thoughts. How many of these interpretations are supported by the evidence in the play? Explain.

6. Do any of Shakespeare's *female* characters fit Northrop Frye's model of the tragic hero? (Lady Macbeth? Ophelia? Cordelia?) How might a feminist theory of tragedy rewrite both Frye and Aristotle? Which characters in which plays would you begin with in order to build a feminist theory of tragedy? Why?

The Tragedies on Film

Unlike the comedies, which focus on groups of stereotypical or stock characters, Shakespeare's tragedies focus on central figures who are deep and complex. They are also analytical and astute commentators on their own experiences. Further, the plots of the major tragedies are open to multiple interpretation because they leave events unresolved. By contrast, the comedies almost always tie things up neatly at the end. For these reasons among others, the tragedies have received substantially more attention from filmmakers over the years than have the comedies. *Hamlet* has been a favorite subject for filmed treatments. Among the other major tragedies, *Romeo and Juliet* and *Othello* have drawn the attention of some of the film industry's best and brightest. And *Macbeth* and *King Lear*, too, have been sensitively re-imagined. Even that bloodiest of Shakespeare's many plays, the revenge tragedy *Titus Andronicus* was brilliantly filmed in 1999—as if to announce that the millennium and Armageddon were cousins.

Consequently, we have multiple film versions of each of these plays. These many film versions make it possible to use a comparative strategy to develop further our critical analysis of Shakespearean tragedy.

Titus Andronicus

Titus Andronicus is almost certainly Shakespeare's earliest tragedy; it may even be his earliest play; it's certainly his most violent play. In recent years, its reputation has gone up (in tandem with that other difficult and rather postmodern play, *Troilus and Cressida*), enough so that nowadays it is showing up much more often on course syllabi at universities. It has even begun to be performed more frequently on stage, usually in repertory or at smaller venues where the intimacy of the setting adds to the intensity, even shock, of the action in the narrative. Julie Taymor's response to Shakespeare's first venture into the subgenre of revenge tragedy (the other—and later excursus—was *Hamlet*) is a truly remarkable film, impressive enough in every way to propel audiences to go (or, in rare cases, go back) to the play with renewed interest and great anticipation. Taymor's oeuvre has crossed between film and stage. She won Tony awards for directing and costume design on the Broadway production of *The Lion King* several years ago. She also directed a 1986 video-release version of *The Tempest* and a 1992 television production of *Oedipus Rex*.

The visual style of *Titus* is stunning, and it clearly shows the influence of Taymor's work on the stage. Many of the costumes are a stylized mixture of Roman, medieval, and punk elements. The sets offer both classical grandeur and post-apocalyptic decay. *Titus* is a feast for cinematography buffs; every single frame is aesthetically composed and polished to a decadent sheen. It doesn't seem as if her *Titus* has kicked off a renaissance of interest in Shakespeare's Roman plays, but it frankly *should* have because it represents a brilliant example of the power of film to re-present one of Shakespeare's lesser-known dramas.

The general impression offered by reviewers at the time the film was released was that Taymor's film was just too much. Roger Ebert terms her version of the play "brilliant and absurd" ("brilliant *because* absurd" would have been better) and continues: the film "goes over the top, doubles back and goes over the top again." He's right, but then that's exactly what the *play* does—only the play is even more repetitively violent than Taymor allows. Wesley Morris, in the *San Francisco Examiner*, argues that Taymor has created "a therapy session that's brutal not just for its graphic horrors." As was Ebert, he's only partly right—about the horrors, yes, but there's no therapy in sight, not even on the distant horizon. Later Morris remarks, "Taymor isn't crafting metaphors here, she's skywriting them." Yes, but we don't understand Morris's tone of disapproval at Taymor's excesses. To her credit, all Taymor does is to find a way to represent grotesque excess on screen; it's certainly in the play itself.

In addition to failing to read the violence in her film accurately, few film critics or scholars note how carefully and cleverly Taymor works with the text itself. An examination of just the first scene in the play (an unusually long Shakespearean opener at 496 lines) shows this. Of the nearly 500 lines, Taymor (she wrote the screenplay as well as directing) cuts about 90, but does so with just a few snips here and there. All the important actions in the scene are shown and dwelled on. (At one point, she even reuses lines for dramatic effect.) Otherwise, she very much leaves Shakespeare's lines alone except to clear up the occasional textual ambiguity arising from the archaic quality of the playwright's language for a contemporary audience. To her credit, Taymor decides to rearrange the sequence of subscenes within the first scene, so that the first 63 lines (which deal with the rivalry between Saturninus and Bassanius) come *after* the triumphal return to Rome of its great leader, Titus Andronicus, and his few remaining sons and not where Shakespeare originally put them: *before*. It's a sign of Shakespeare's relative immaturity, in fact, that he didn't see the dramatic weaknesses that result from interrupting the political infighting with Titus's military exploits.

Along the way, Taymor shows a rare talent for the arresting image: the mud-covered soldiers entering the coliseum in robotic marching formation; the eerie even sickening combination of ancient weapons and modern artillery; the ritualistic shower which the Andronicii take to cleanse themselves of the horror of war; Tamora's sorrowful, tear-stained face seen through the flames of the fire; the animal-head

91

statuary above Saturninus's throne; the decadent party which the new emperor throws for his guests to show his power. Indeed, we think that Taymor only makes one mistake (in the first scene and—by extension—throughout the play): she uses a framing device of a boy playing with soldiers. He shows up not just at the beginning of the film either (in an opening sequence that runs almost 3 minutes) but hangs around the action like the sorest of thumbs getting in the way of the action's immediacy. We know, of course, what point Taymor is making; it's the equivalent of Buffy Sainte Marie's classic anti-war song, "Universal Soldier." However, she's making it at tremendous dramatic cost and without Bertolt Brecht's excuse of aiming for an Alienation Effect. She may have picked this idea up from the 1985 BBC/Time-Life production of the play; if so, she should have left it by the side of the road.

That's our sole major concern about her wonderful film. One could quibble about her use of saxophonists at the party scene as being jarring; one could complain that she tips her hand too early about the relation between the captured Goth queen, Tamora, and Aaron, a Moor and her lover. We even feel that Tamora's gold breastplate is a little too much (over the top?) because it seems as if it's wearing her. This, however, is all minor caviling, for Taymor does a stunning job of driving home Shakespeare's insight: violence breeds violence (of course), but violence also destroys any and all possibility of moral redemption (not quite so obvious).

Analysis and Interpretation: Taymor's Titus

1. One of the most notable aspects of *Titus* is its highly aestheticized presentation of violence. Does Taymor's aesthetic distance viewers from the impact of the violence of the play? Does the violence serve a purpose in the film? Does the film offer any hope for redemption or escape from the cyclical ritual of violence and retribution?

2. One critic writes, "The film production is marked by gross indulgence and hideous excess, but it is sometimes shockingly effective and even darkly humorous" (Welsh, Vela, and Tibbetts 101). What evidence of "dark humor" do you find in *Titus*?

3. What kinds of framing devices does Taymor employ in her film? How does the opening, where young Lucius plays with his toy soldiers, function as a frame? What does young Lucius discover or learn in the course of the film's story?

Romeo and Juliet

Romeo and Juliet is a tragedy with a double focus: on the star-crossed young lovers and on their families, whose "ancient grudge" boils over into "new mutiny" and brings grief to the people of Verona (Prologue 3). The tragedy comes with the lesson that only through the death of the lovers and the sadness that ensues can wisdom be achieved. This tragic recognition comes to the Capulet and Montague families as the Friar retells the story of Romeo and Juliet's "misadventured, piteous overthrows" (Prologue 7). They realize their own complicity in the deaths of their children, but that realization comes too late.

Romeo and Juliet does not precisely fit the classical Aristotelian definition of tragedy discussed earlier. As tragic protagonists, Romeo and Juliet lack stature and depth; they are very young (in their early teens), and are typical teenagers in many ways—including their passionate attachment to one another. The major obstacle to their love comes from their parents, but such an obstacle is typical of the domestic comedies of Shakespeare's early career rather than of the tragedies of his later phase. The tragic recognition so important in Aristotle's view of tragedy is not something they themselves experience because they are already dead by the time it occurs. The recognition comes instead to their parents, and by extension to the community of Verona, when it becomes clear that the young lovers have died because of a continuing cycle of violence and revenge that infects the city.

Like many of the comedies (but few of the tragedies), *Romeo and Juliet* ends with the restoration of order. Capulet and Montague, grieving for the loss of their children, at last put an end to their strife with a ceremonial public handshake that closes the play in a mood described by the Chorus as "a gloomy peace" (5.3.305). The play shares both comic and tragic elements, then. The theme of young love suddenly flowering despite parental opposition links it to comedies such as *A Midsummer Night's Dream* while the tragic cycle of violence that exacts the price of the young couple's death renders the comic elements tragic with poignant and bittersweet overtones. *Romeo and Juliet* is not the dark tragedy of *Othello.* Instead, it involves the exquisite agony of youthful passion, the flame that burns so brightly only because it will fade so fast.

The Chorus, who opens the play, tells us how things are going to end and, by such a foreshadowing, adds an aura of inevitability to the plot (Prologue 1–14). From the beginning, the lovers are identified as "star-crossed," and we are told that "with their death" they will "bury their parents' strife." Is their death inevitable, however? What does it mean that they are "star-crossed"? As with many of the tragedies, there is a balance between fate and human agency in *Romeo and Juliet.* Structurally, the play suggests the feud between the Montagues and Capulets is a primary cause of the tragedy: The first scene is a street fight, and the Chorus comments that family enmity is the main reason for the lovers' deaths. Yet both chance and human actions do play a part in the outcome as well: letters are not delivered in time; Romeo rashly chooses to duel with Tybalt even though he knows he is risking death or banishment.

Two major films have been made of *Romeo and Juliet,* each a serious effort to make the story speak to a new generation. Franco Zeffirelli's 1968 film was self-consciously crafted to appeal to the youth culture of the 1960s. Baz Luhrmann's 1996 film, *William Shakespeare's Romeo + Juliet* brought a postmodern sensibility and a frenetic visual style to grab the attention of the media-savvy youth of the 1990s.

Zeffirelli's *Romeo and Juliet* (1968)

Franco Zeffirelli's film of *Romeo and Juliet* was released in 1968. That date coincided with the Vietnam war and was a time when the emergent youth culture of the 1960s was articulating an ethos of passion, love, and peace against an older generation's conservatism and militarism. The cultural conflicts of that era matched the theme of generational conflict in Shakespeare's text, and Zeffirelli's film self-consciously highlighted these connections. Zeffirelli chose to use actors (Leonard Whiting and Olivia Hussey) who were young and relatively unknown, so audiences would be able to see them as the teenage lovers with little or no preconceptions. This strategy was almost the direct opposite of his earlier decision to cast Elizabeth Taylor and Richard Burton in his 1967 *Taming of the Shrew*. (See Chapter 2.) Where the audience for *Taming* would naturally see Taylor and Burton first and Kate and Petruchio second, the audience for *Romeo and Juliet* would see not the actors but only the characters.

Zeffirelli's film is visually stunning. It was filmed in coastal Italian towns that look like fifteenth-century Verona. The costumes and sets are lush, detailed, and authentic. The film, not surprisingly, won Academy Awards for cinematography and costume. The film opens with a sweeping high shot overlooking Verona, a shot that echoes the opening sequence of Laurence Olivier's 1944 *Henry V*. (See Chapter 1.) In *Romeo and Juliet*, it is in fact the voice of Olivier himself that delivers the opening Chorus as a voice-over as the camera pans across the cityscape. As the camera descends into the city, we find ourselves in a crowded, bustling, dusty marketplace replete with onions and peppers ripening on vendors' wagons. The Capulet boys appear in bright red and yellow velvet suits; the Montagues follow soon afterwards in dark greens and blues. The costumes lend even the fight scenes a feeling of summer warmth and sensuality. Zeffirelli's visual style in the film might be called heightened realism. The settings are realistic, and the costuming and locations are all historically authentic and believable. The result is to translate the play fully into film. Zeffirelli presents Shakespeare's play as an actual event unfolding before our eyes rather than as a staged drama.

Zeffirelli's desire to bring a new audience to the play may have contributed to his streamlined script. Only about one third of the play's text remains, and many of Zeffirelli's cuts work to create more simplified and one-dimensional versions of the lead characters. Zeffirelli's Romeo and Juliet are less reflective and philosophical than Shakespeare's, but they nonetheless resonated with the youthful film audience of 1968. That audience made the film one of the most popular and successful Shakespeare-based films of all time.

Analysis and Interpretation: Zeffirelli's Romeo and Juliet

1. How does Zeffirelli present the relationship between Romeo and Juliet? What kind of body language and nonverbal cues does he employ to suggest the nature of their relationship? How does his screenplay edit and reshape their lines to present them to a film audience?

2. Does Zeffirelli's film suggest that fate plays a role in the lovers' deaths? To what extent are the lovers shown in his version to be part of a larger process or cycle of violence? How is their tragedy explained or understood by the characters around them? What other explanations for the tragedy does the film offer? How much does chance play a role? Do any of the characters exhibit any tragic flaws? How are these shown in the film?

3. Many critics have seen in this film echoes of the generation gap characteristic of popular culture in the 1960s. What evidence do you see of these echoes in the film? What kind of social commentary do you think Zeffirelli is offering through his choice of Shakespeare's tragedy of love? What choices does Zeffirelli make as a director to reinforce his commentary?

4. How does Zeffirelli's film present the Montague and Capulet parents? Are they effective role models? What part do they play in the film and the outcome of the action? What kind of spin is put on them as parents and role models? What are their own marriages like?

5. By presenting a more accessible and streamlined version of Shakespeare, has Zeffirelli gone too far in his efforts to popularize the play for a 1960s audience? What is lost in his translation to the medium of film? What is gained by his editing and visual style?

Luhrmann's *William Shakespeare's Romeo + Juliet* (1996)

A glance at the names of some of the characters in the cast for Baz Luhrmann's 1996 version of *Romeo and Juliet* suggests how Luhrmann has updated the play for a new youth culture Lord Montague has become "Ted," and the Chorus is now identified as a TV "Anchorwoman." Like Franco Zeffirelli in the 1960s, Luhrmann has devised a filmmaking strategy based on an explicit desire to merge Shakespeare's play with contemporary youth culture. Luhrmann sets his film in the present, in a society populated with gun-toting gangs and heavily armed police helicopters patrolling the lawless streets. Luhrmann's editing is fast-paced, and the visual style of the film is vibrant and excessive, full of both pop-culture icons and religious symbols.

With John Leguizamo as Tybalt, in a setting that evokes a blend of Miami, Los Angeles, and Rio de Janeiro, the film has a distinctively Latin rather than Italian flavor. The Latin Capulets are countered by the Anglo Montagues. African Americans are cast in mediating roles (Mercutio and Captain Prince, most notably). So, the issues of race and ethnicity are layered onto the family conflicts present in Shakespeare's play. We cannot help but see symbolic meanings in the film; we are asked to see it as an indirect commentary on gang violence and racial conflict. The popularity of the film suggests it is an effective one.

Shakespeare's Verona has become Luhrmann's Verona Beach, a sultry city at once opulent and run-down. Here is the way one setting, a downtrodden beach-front amusement park, is described by Luhrmann and his co-author, Craig Pearce, in their screenplay:

EXT. BEACH. DAWN.

To the melancholic strains of Mozart's "Serenade for Winds," we discover the ornate arch of what is left of a once splendid cinema. At the top of the arch the words "Sycamore Grove" are clearly visible. The cinema has been demolished but for its proscenium, through which we can see the grubby shore of Verona Beach, housing a collection of sex clubs and strip joints, populated with prostitutes, drag queens, clients, and street people. (17)

Towering over this street scene are three symbolic structures that function as icons throughout the film. Two high-rise chrome-and-steel buildings loom above opposite ends of the street. Each is adorned with a huge lighted sign, one reading "Montague" and the other "Capulet." The two rival families are refigured in Luhrmann's film as mega-corporations dominating the landscape of Verona Beach much as they dominate its economy. The third symbol is religious, a giant statue of Jesus that looks very much like the famous real-life statue of Christ, arms outspread, that overlooks the city of Rio de Janeiro in Brazil. The camera returns to this statue repeatedly throughout the film, and religions icons appear in many other scenes as well: from a church filled with blue neon crosses at Juliet's funeral to the tiny cross she wears around her neck.

In the preface to the screenplay, Luhrmann writes: "We're trying to make this movie rambunctious, sexy, violent, and entertaining in the way Shakespeare might have if he had been a filmmaker. We have not shied away from clashing low comedy with high tragedy, which is the style of the play, for it's the low comedy that allows you to embrace the very high emotions of the tragedy" (vi). Luhrmann retains Shakespeare's original language, however. In doing so, this film does not become *West Side Story* but remains recognizable as *Romeo and Juliet* even though transplanted to a contemporary setting. Luhrmann's intentions are clear enough: his goal is to create a Shakespeare for the masses by putting together a modern film tragedy that a wide range of audiences can understand and enjoy. Yet, he wants to do so in the language of Shakespeare.

Analysis and Interpretation: Luhrmann's William Shakespeare's Romeo + Juliet

1. Luhrmann chooses to update the setting of *Romeo and Juliet* to the present day and yet at the same time to retain Shakespeare's language. What effect does the Shakespearean language and stylized dialogue have on the film? How would the film be different if the language were updated to contemporary English?

2. Keep track of the religious iconography and symbolism used throughout the film. What are their functions? Is this a religious

film? Do you think the religious imagery heightens or emphasizes a religious theme? Why or why not?

3. Look carefully at the ending of Luhrmann's film. How is it different from Shakespeare's? What effect do these differences have on the tone of the film?

4. Luhrmann uses the framing device of television news coverage as a way of remaking the Chorus for a contemporary context. One reviewer has suggested that this makes his film "darker" than Zeffirelli's because Romeo and Juliet become just another news story—another tragedy getting its 15 minutes of fame only to be forgotten. Do you agree with this interpretation? How do you think the news-story framework functions in the film?

5. Make a log of the different camera angles and shots used in Luhrmann's film. Notice the diverse range of shots used, from high overhead (helicopter) views to extreme close-ups. The camera seems to move in and out of the scenes from many angles and directions. Where are we positioned as viewers by Luhrmann's camera and editing? Are we encouraged to share the world of the two lovers? Are we outside looking in? Or is something else going on? How does Luhrmann use the camera to create and establish our relationship to the actors? To the story?

6. Is there any change in the pacing and style of the shots when the camera is focused on the two young lovers? How does the film create a sense of intimacy with and closeness to these characters?

7. Is Luhrmann's film still a tragedy in the sense Shakespeare would have understood? Has the story become something else entirely in its new setting and with its visual style? What is tragic about Luhrmann's film? How is his sense of tragedy similar to and different from Shakespeare's? How does Luhrmann's sense of tragedy compare to Zeffirelli's?

Hamlet

If the substantial history of *Hamlet* on film is any indication, Shakespeare's most famous tragedy is something of a Rorschach test for directors. *Hamlet* is like an inkblot on a page, and interpreting the blot says more about the interpreter than it does about the inkblot. Laurence Olivier's 1948 *Hamlet*, for example, has been seen as the most "Freudian" and psychological interpretation of the play. Kenneth Branagh's 1996 version is the most obsessive and perfectionist, for it keeps virtually every line of the original play intact and, so, delivers a 242-minute epic version of Shakespeare's longest play. Branagh's *Hamlet* is also, perhaps, the most political of the cinematic versions. Interpreting Hamlet (the character *and* the play) seems to be something filmmakers love and need to do. They have provided students of the play with a stunning variety of visual narratives to add to the existing storehouse of critical knowledge about this great tragedy. All of Shakespeare's tragedies can be interpreted in multiple ways, but none more so than *Hamlet*. The diverse range of different film treatments bears ample witness to this fact. We'll focus here on the four most widely available and markedly different feature-film versions: Olivier's, Zeffirelli's (starring Mel Gibson in 1991), Branagh's, and Michael Almereyda's (set in contemporary Manhattan and starring Ethan Hawke).

Olivier's *Hamlet* (1948)

Laurence Olivier's 1948 black-and-white *Hamlet* is perhaps the most influential Shakespeare film ever as well as the most influential interpretation of the play. The entire film seems to be shrouded in fog and deep shadows, and Olivier's Castle Elsinore is mazelike, stony, and cold. In this way, Olivier establishes an atmosphere of alienation, isolation, despair. The visual style of Olivier's film owes much to the *film noir* genre. Its ethos works in Olivier's film to highlight the corruption of the Danish court and, at the same time, to contribute to the atmosphere of mystery, intrigue, and surveillance in the play.

Olivier's film establishes a strong, individualized interpretation of the play right from the very beginning. The film opens with these lines printed on the screen; they appear before us as Olivier reads them aloud in a voice-over::

> So, oft it chances in particular men,
> That for some vicious mole of nature in them,

By their o'ergrowth of some complexion,
Oft breaking down the pales and forts of reason,
Or by some habit grown too much; that these men—
Carrying, I say, the stamp of one defect,
Their virtues else—be they as pure as grace,
Shall in the general censure take corruption
From that particular fault.

                    (1.4.23–35)

Olivier's opening voice-over concludes with the following statement: "This is the tragedy of a man who could not make up his mind." This line is of course Olivier's and not Shakespeare's, and, coupled with the opening speech just quoted, it establishes a fixed interpretive framework for the play. The lines above are taken from Act 1, Scene 4, in which Hamlet is commenting on the excessive drinking and revelry of the new King Claudius and his court. Taken out of context and used at the beginning of the film, the lines appear to describe Hamlet himself. You can compare Olivier's edited version of the soliloquy to the original text (1.4.23–36) to see how Olivier's changes also shift the meaning of the passage.

The interpretation of *Hamlet* as being about indecision or inaction is only partially correct. It's possible to read Hamlet's delay and patience as a calculating and, indeed, effective strategy rather than as a central tragic flaw in his character. Nevertheless, Olivier's reading of the play as presented in this influential film has surely had an effect on generations of filmmakers and probably some teachers and students of *Hamlet* as well. Olivier's screenplay cuts just over half of the text, and omits several characters, including Rosencrantz and Guildenstern. The entire Fortinbras subplot is also cut from Olivier's film so that a significant political dimension is erased.

Olivier himself described his film as an "essay in Hamlet" and not as a film version of the play. He wrote: "I feel it is misleading to couple Shakespeare's play with the film of *Hamlet*, and for this reason. In Shakespeare's play, as in all his plays, there runs a beautifully intricate and complete pattern of character and action. The only satisfactory way of appreciating all that Shakespeare meant by *Hamlet* is to sit down in a theater and follow a performance of the great play in its entirety" (Behrens and Rosen 748). Despite this disclaimer, it's still very interesting to look at Olivier's film in the context of the play's text to see what the great actor and filmmaker chose to dwell on in his presentation of the tragedy.

Analysis and Interpretation: Olivier's Hamlet

1. Olivier made a conscious choice to film his *Hamlet* in black and white. He wanted the whole film to be in muted tones (in stark contrast to his extremely colorful *Henry V*, filmed four years earlier, in 1944; see Chapter 3). How do you think the black-and-white photography contributes to the emotional effect of the film? How would it be different if it were filmed in color?

2. Olivier uses a number of camera techniques to represent his idea of *Hamlet* visually. There are many deep focus shots. There are moments (when Hamlet sees the ghost of his father, for example) when the camera blurs in and out of focus to the rhythm of a beating heart. In other scenes, the camera hovers high above the actors on the set. Olivier also frequently uses doorways and archways visually to frame and separate the actors in particular scenes. Watch carefully for these and other camera techniques and make a list of distinctive shots. How do these shots affect the look and effect of specific scenes in the film?

3. How does Olivier's decision to focus on *Hamlet* as a psychological drama affect your view of the play? What does he show about Hamlet's character, motivation, or personality that helps you to understand him better? How do you understand Olivier's interpretation of the play as "the tragedy of a man who could not make up his mind"? What does such an interpretation distort or leave out?

4. Do some background reading to learn more about *film noir*. How does Olivier's film exhibit some of the visual and narrative characteristics of the genre? Critics have also noted the use of "expressionistic" techniques. What is German expressionism in film? How does Olivier's film exemplify expressionist techniques and strategies?

Zeffirellli's *Hamlet* (1991)

Olivier's 1948 *Hamlet* so dominated the cinematic landscape that it was over 40 years before another major feature film was made of the play. (A low-budget version of the play, directed by Tony Richardson, was distributed by Columbia Pictures in 1969, but only in limited release; for details, see the filmography in the Additional Resources at the back of this book.) Zeffirelli's decision to cast action-hero Mel Gibson in the lead caused some consternation to put it mildly, but the film was considered to be surprisingly successful both critically and financially. As he did with *Romeo and Juliet*, Zeffirelli creates in his *Hamlet* a visual feast of detailed costumes and wonderful set designs. His Elsinore is almost medieval, more primitive, besmirched, and earthy than Olivier's (and certainly a stark contrast to Branagh's film with its use of the opulent Blenheim Palace as Elsinore). Casting Gibson and Glenn Close (as Gertrude) certainly attracted audiences to the theater who might not otherwise have gone to see a Shakespeare film. Zeffirelli's version of the play can be viewed as an effective attempt to produce a relatively accessible and popular film of *Hamlet*. Gibson's Hamlet may not offer the psychological depth and introspection of Olivier's, but it may well be the case that his performance is more understandable and perhaps equally moving for many filmgoers.

In an interview after the film's release, Zeffirelli confessed that one reason he had wanted to cast Gibson as Hamlet was his voice—"I was madly in love with his voice" (Behrens and Rosen 763). Indeed, Zeffirelli admits that voice and language are the most important and difficult aspects in filming Shakespeare, and his hope is that "in making it [a soliloquy] clear to himself, Mel helps others to understand it better" (764). Gibson's muted Australian accent does make for good listening, so you may feel more compassion and understanding for his Hamlet than for Olivier's more stagy and theatrical presentation.

Zeffirelli also said some interesting things about his use of color and its relationship to the setting and themes of *Hamlet*. "I keyed the whole movie to mostly grays and ash colors, a 'medieval-primitive' look, the look of a society that is brutal and made of stone. Whenever a few rich colors do come out, the effect is even more vivid. In that sense, this is one of the most colorful films I've ever done—but only because the few rich colors stand out so much from the grays" (764). Zeffirelli's visual style in some ways echoes Olivier's and in other ways departs from it, and the effect of his use of color is indeed striking.

In stark contrast to Olivier's use of *film noir*, Zeffirelli draws instead on action-adventure conventions and styles. The choice of Mel Gibson for the lead role clearly reinforces this genre distinction—it would be impossible for audiences *not* to think of *Mad Max* and *Lethal Weapon* when they saw Gibson as the Danish prince. This distinction is emphasized too by the drastic cuts made to the text of the play. Many lines are acted or expressed nonverbally rather than spoken. Here is the way one critic summarizes these stylistic differences and their effect on the way we see and respond to Hamlet: "Olivier's direction emphasizes Hamlet's entrapment; close-ups stress his inwardness and long shots make him seem diminished and isolated in the context of Elsinore. Left to his own devices, Olivier's Hamlet would decline and die of grief. Gibson's Hamlet snarls; low-angle shots and vibrant close-ups make him dominate each moment on screen" (Keyishian 78).

Analysis and Interpretation: Zeffirelli's Hamlet

1. Zeffirelli makes a number of cuts to Shakespeare's text to get his film down to a running time of 135 minutes. Make a list of key scenes or lines that Zeffirelli has cut from his screenplay. What does his strategy seem to be for such cuts? What criteria has he used in deciding what to keep and what to leave out? How does his editing strategy compare to Olivier's?

2. How does Zeffirelli's film portray Hamlet's relationships to his mother and to Ophelia? Does Gibson's Hamlet sexualize his relationships to women? To what extent do sexuality and femininity (or a fear of feminine sexuality) play a part in his character? How would you outline a feminist interpretation of Zeffirelli's film?

3. To what extent do you think Zeffirelli has succeeded in his goal of creating a more accessible and popular *Hamlet* for contemporary audiences? What does it help you to see about Hamlet's character and his motivations? Do you think the film would make sense for audiences who have not read the play? Is that important? Why?

4. Find examples of scenes that Zeffirelli has invented or added (such as the funeral scene at the beginning, for example). What is the effect of such inventions and additions? Look at the way Zeffirelli stages the major soliloquies as well. How is his visual and narrative presentation different from Olivier's? What effect do these differences have on your experience and understanding of the play?

Branagh's *Hamlet* (1996)

If Zeffirelli's is a populist's *Hamlet*, Branagh's film could be described as a purist's. The 1996 film includes (almost) every line from Shakespeare's play. It stays methodically close to the text and has very few cuts, abridgements, or rearrangements of scenes or even individual lines. As a result, Branagh's film runs 242 minutes, just over four hours. If you watch Branagh's film after Olivier's or Zeffirelli's, you'll be struck by the substantial differences, not only in the length and leisureliness of the scenes but also in the feel and texture of the film as a whole. Branagh's version seems much more concerned with the political and social world that hems in Hamlet. Fortinbras and the approach of his army towards Elsinore drive the plot along, and the modern-era military feel of the film is notably different from the medieval symbolism and psychology of both Olivier's and Zeffirelli's interpretations of this iconic work.

In terms of genre, Branagh's film borrows much from the epic tradition of *Gone with the Wind, Ben Hur*, and *Doctor Zhivago*. This apparent borrowing is, in part, simply a function of length—at more than four hours Branagh's *Hamlet* is inevitably a different kind of cinematic experience from the two-hour versions by Olivier and Zeffirelli. As one critic puts it, "Epic films tend to be paced majestically, prizing plenitude and variety over compactness and consistency of tone. Events tend to be broken up into episodes that are linked but self-contained, and enacted in a wide assortment of places" (Keyishian 78). The sharp narrative focus of the Olivier and Zeffirelli versions of the play disappears in Branagh's epic, but the verbal abundance of Shakespeare's play and its rich intertextuality are regained. Other film conventions typical of the epic are in evidence in Branagh's film as well. Flashbacks are used in several instances to show audiences visually what a character is remembering or retelling in a speech. The most notable examples of this technique are the flashbacks of Hamlet and Ophelia in bed together, for these make it explicit for audiences (even if Shakespeare does not) that the two have indeed been romantically and sexually involved.

If we have any doubts that Branagh's film draws on the conventions of the epic, his treatment of the "How all occasions do inform against me" soliloquy (4.4.34–67) should be enough to convince us. Branagh delivers the speech from a snowy, windswept mountain ridge with a craggy rim of peaks behind him in the distance. The entire scene is white with snow and cold with wind, and as he delivers the lines the camera begins to pull back slowly from a tight focus to extreme wide angle. By the end of the speech, Hamlet is a tiny black speck against a sweeping landscape of mountainous white. This shot tells us that whatever else he may be, Hamlet is but a man, a tiny being in a vast world. Symphonic music rises, and as Hamlet delivers the final lines, the kettle drums throb—"My thoughts be bloody or be nothing worth!"—and we fade to black, and to Intermission. This speech, deleted from many film and stage performances, becomes the turning point of Branagh's film on both a dramatic and a cinematic level.

The set design and visual style of Branagh's film are markedly different from both Olivier's and Zeffirelli's versions as well. Branagh's Elsinore is the real-world Blenheim Palace, an eighteenth-century country house (residence of the Duke of Marlborough) that is opulent and splendid. This choice goes some way to dictating the costumes, which are nineteenth century and heavily militarized, and the props: muskets and cannon as well as swords and rapiers. Blenheim is filled with mirrors, and Branagh even films the "To be or not to be" soliloquy with Hamlet standing in front of a mirror. The mirrors signal both self-consciousness and surveillance: In one scene, Hamlet confronts Ophelia knowing that Polonius is watching from behind a mirrored door. He even presses her face into the two-way glass once he has opened and searched behind every door *but one*. Branagh's Elsinore is rich, gaudy, proud, and undeniably corrupt.

An intriguing visual device frames the film: At the beginning of the film, the camera lingers over the pedestal of a large stone statue of the late King Hamlet. We return to this statue again at the end of the film as Fortinbras's soldiers tear it down. The last image of the film is the head of King Hamlet as it tumbles from the statue. This visual device echoes not only Shelley's famous sonnet "Ozymandias" (with its poignant recognition that even the greatest monuments of the most powerful erode away over eons) but also the toppling of statues of Lenin all over Russia at the fall of the Soviet Union in 1989–1990. It also eerily foreshadows the toppling of Saddam Hussein's statue in Baghdad in April 2003. Branagh seems to use this image to link his *Hamlet* to the larger cycles of human history and cyclic change in order to suggest, perhaps, that another epoch is beginning with the rise of Fortinbras.

Analysis and Interpretation: Branagh's Hamlet

1. Unlike any of the other *Hamlet* films, Branagh's film uses the complete Shakespeare text (with a few minor cuts *and* additions). Which scenes stand out for you when you watch this film alongside the others? How does your view of the play and its central dramas change with the inclusion of these scenes?

2. Critic Harry Keyishian writes of Branagh's use of epic conventions: "This *Hamlet*, to be sure, is not reflective of the early epic, which tends to celebrate national values and aspirations, but rather of a later, revisionist kind, full of subversive ironies and demythification" (80). What subversive ironies and demythification do you find in Branagh's film? How does it compare to a nationalistic film such Olivier's *Henry V*? Does Branagh manage to combine epic filmmaking with Shakespearean tragedy? In what ways? Is his film still a tragedy, in

either an Aristotelian or Shakespearean sense, or has it become something different?

3. Besides the obvious symbolism of the large statue of King Hamlet that begins and ends the film, what other key symbols or motifs does Branagh use? Make a list of the key symbols and motifs you find, and compare them to Olivier's or Zeffirelli's. What differences do you find? What is the significance of these differences?

4. Here is how Kenneth Branagh himself describes his filmmaking strategy for *Hamlet*: "The screenplay is what one might call the 'verbal storyboard.' An inflexion of a subjective view of the play which has developed over the years. Its intention was to be both personal, with enormous attention paid to the intimate relations between the characters, and at the same time epic, with a sense of the country at large and of a dynasty in decay" (Behrens and Rosen 786). What parts of the film are "intimate"? Which are "epic"? How do Branagh's strategies compare to those of other filmmakers? Is his juxtaposition of the personal and the political stories effective? Is it more authentic or true to the play? Why or why not?

5. Roger Ebert compared Branagh's *Hamlet* to Olivier's in a January 1997 review of the Branagh film: "Branagh's *Hamlet* lacks the narcissistic intensity of Laurence Olivier's . . . but the film as a whole is better, placing Hamlet in the larger context of royal politics, and making him less a subject for pity" (Behrens and Rosen 788). Do you agree with Ebert's comparisons? What evidence from the two films supports his observations? What evidence might you use to construct a counterargument?

Almereyda's *Hamlet* (2000)

Michael Almereyda has been described as the archetypal indie filmmaker. He produces low-budget, art-house films outside the major film-studio circuit. His films before he made *Hamlet* include *Another Girl, Another Planet* (1994) and *Nadja* (1995), the latter being about a vampire in Manhattan. Both films were produced using toy cameras on miniscule budgets, and both became cult hits (Behrens and Rosen 816). Almereyda seems to be in unusual company in the context of monumental Shakespearean greats such as Laurence Olivier or massive studio budgets such as that enjoyed by Kenneth Branagh for *Hamlet*. Yet his *Hamlet*, set in contemporary New York City and starring Ethan Hawke and Julia Stiles (who appears, incidentally, in two other Shakespeare-inspired films: *10 Things I Hate about You* and *O*), is a haunting and effective take on *Hamlet* in a postmodern techno-thriller setting.

By placing the film in a present-day context, Almereyda is able to make explicit the links between the corruption of the Danish court and modern corporations. Denmark has become Denmark Corporation, with Kyle MacLachlan as CEO Claudius challenged by renegade upstart Fortinbras. The proxy fight over the chairmanship of the corporation is chronicled in the pages of *USA Today*, pages Claudius ceremoniously rips to pieces before his assembled shareholders as he announces his new position and his new wife, Gertrude. Elsinore Castle becomes the Elsinore Hotel, complete with video surveillance cameras that capture images of the ghost of Hamlet's father (played by Sam Shepard) as he walks through the laundry room and across the balconies high above Times Square.

Most importantly, the contemporary setting allows Almereyda to introduce the theme of technology as a mediating force in human relationships. Hamlet, for example, is now a budding amateur filmmaker himself. Instead of the play-within-the-play, in Almereyda's film we get a *film* within the play. *The Mousetrap* is "a film/video by Hamlet," and we see Hamlet at work editing and filming throughout the action. Several major soliloquies are spoken into the camera or are replayed on a grainy digital monitor. Answering machines and faxes also serve as postmodern messengers in the film. Almereyda suggests the extraordinary degree to which all our interactions and communications are now mediated by machines. Hamlet even delivers his "get thee to a nunnery" speech to Ophelia on her answering machine.

Despite the high-tech gadgets and the contemporary setting, Almereyda's film uses Shakespeare's original language throughout. It may strike some viewers as odd or jarring to hear Hamlet speaking

109

Elizabethan English while walking around Manhattan, but the effect in fact highlights the language and effectively draws attention to the speech patterns. In one tongue-in-cheek scene, Hamlet delivers his "To be or not to be" soliloquy as he wanders through the aisles of a Blockbuster video outlet. The category sign visible on the shelf behind him reads "ACTION."

Analysis and Interpretation: Almereyda's Hamlet

1. One reviewer of Almereyda's film, Alexandra Marshall, comments that Almereyda's women characters are deeper and more interesting than in any other film version of *Hamlet*: "Julia Stiles . . . embodies Ophelia with an authenticity equal to Diane Venora's Gertrude. In this film, we truly experience Ophelia's madness as the high-cost consequence of her insight. . . . This Gertrude and Ophelia . . . make us aware of how much of the story we have missed in less 'modernized' *Hamlet*s with their unexplored women" (Behrens and Rosen 830–831). Compare the presentation of Gertrude and Ophelia in this film with the way they are portrayed in the other three *Hamlet* films discussed in this chapter. What evidence do you find to support Marshall's claim? What evidence might challenge or modify her assertions? Are the modern female characters more powerful and more developed? In what ways? Which representation seems most satisfying to you? Why?

2. Make a list of all the different uses and representations of technology and gadgetry in Almereyda's film. How do these devices function? What do they add to the story? Why and how?

3. Ethan Hawke is the youngest actor among the four who play Hamlet in the films we've been discussing here. How does his performance compare to the others? Do you like his Hamlet? How would you describe his style? What sides of Hamlet's character does Hawke want to show us? Is his Hamlet more or less likable than the others? Why?

4. Notice how Almereyda's editing and cutting breaks up some of the scenes and interpolates them into other scenes. Sometimes a line or two from one scene repeats on a video monitor in the

background or foreground of another scene. How does this contemporary crosscutting method work? Does it disrupt or support the dramatic narrative of the play? Does it do both?

Othello

Othello is Shakespeare's exploration of jealousy (specifically sexual jealousy) and its destructive power. In contrast to the broad scope and political context of *Hamlet*, the scope and context of *Othello* are relatively small. Its action is intensely focused on the three central characters: Othello, Iago, Desdemona. Layered onto Shakespeare's exploration of the theme of sexual jealousy is a subtext focused on race. Iago uses Othello's blackness against him by suggesting that it would only be "natural" for a white woman such as Desdemona to want the company of a man of her own race after "experimenting" with a black lover and husband. The explicitly racist language of some scenes has limited modern productions of the play or has sometimes required radical rewriting. However, the narrative of the play depends heavily on the power of these racial stereotypes, both as they eat away at Othello's peace of mind and as they circulate through the language of the play. One recent production actually foregrounds the issue of race in the play with a role reversal in which Patrick Stewart plays a white Othello with an all-black supporting cast. Because of its disturbing rhetoric, *Othello* continues to be relevant to modern audiences and contemporary concerns about racial and gender conflict.

Orson Welles' *Othello* (1952)

Orson Welles' 1952 production of *Othello* was remastered with restored sound and music tracks in 1992 and is now, fortunately for us, available on DVD. Filmed in Italy and Morocco in high-contrast black and white, the film is a powerful, poetic, filmic interpretation of Shakespeare's play. From its opening funeral procession, the film is always taut and haunting, for it creates a pervasive tension which it supports with a vibrant, incantatory vocal soundtrack. Welles uses repeated visual imagery, too, of cages, dungeons, and labyrinths to evoke the self-imposed isolation and confusion of Othello's mental landscape.

Welles employs some prose narration through voice-over to fill in the backstory and make room for a more intense focus on crucial scenes. His camera work and editing suggest discontinuity and disruption by making heavy use of montage theories of layering and the juxtaposition of images. As in many of his other films, he makes use of low-angle shots to make figures loom menacingly over viewers. Rarely, in fact, do we look *down* on Othello until the very last scene. Welles' visual style tends to dwell on the architecture of the Italian and Moroccan castles he uses for his sets; in one amazing scene, the Cassio—Roderigo swordfight, the scene is filmed from a reflecting pool in a dramatic symmetry suggestive of the artwork of M. C. Escher.

Oliver Parker's *Othello* (1995)

Contrary to popular belief, this most recent major film version of *Othello* was *not* directed by Kenneth Branagh. Despite the powerful presence of Branagh in the film as Iago, the film was in fact directed by Oliver Parker. Parker's rich colors, realistic sets and more traditional camera work contrast vividly with Orson Welles' heavily stylized and expressionistic version of the play. Laurence Fishburne gives a moving and resonant performance as Othello, one which matches Branagh's sinister embodiment of Iago.

Analysis and Interpretation: Welles' and Parker's Othello

1. Compare the camera techniques of Welles and Parker. Notice the frequent use of low-angle shots and deep focus by Welles. How do these techniques create an emotional effect for Welles' film? How does Parker create a deeper sense of realism in contrast to Welles' more artistic style?

2. How are women portrayed in each film? Look carefully at Emilia's speech to Desdemona about women's capacity for unfaithfulness. Are the female characters more powerful in one film than in the other? How are they different?

3. Both films cut lines and scenes to compress the overall length. What strategies do the directors use in making these cuts? Which film offers a more effective version of the play? How and why?

4. Orson Welles is a white man playing Othello in blackface. Laurence Fishburne is a popular African American actor now known to screen audiences for his work in *The Matrix* films. How are your perceptions of the main character in part responses to these actors and their performances? Is it possible for a white actor to give a convincing performance in a role such as Othello? Is this question at all parallel to the issue of white artists performing hip-hop music? How about white audiences listening to hip-hop? How do contemporary debates about race in popular culture influence your interpretation of these two films? Would a white actor try to play Othello today? Should he? Why or why not?

King Lear

King Lear is the third in Shakespeare's tetralogy of masterworks. It dates from 1605–1606. The tragedy is different from *Hamlet* (existential dread) and from *Othello* (corrosive jealousy). Now we have another human failing writ large: foolishness. King Lear is not a bad man, just a stupid and obstinate one. It makes sense for him to wish to retire in old age, but his wish to retain his authority after having divided up his kingdom and ceded his power makes no sense whatsoever. Worse, in all his obduracy he banishes his beloved daughter when she refuses to flatter him. There have been no recent feature films made of this play. Is its message simply too grim? We do, however, have a wealth of versions to choose from which were originally done for TV or went straight to DVD. By our count, ten can readily been rented or bought including Ernest C. Warde's neglected silent three-reeler from 1916 and Grigori Kosintsev's Russian-language version, *Korol Lir*. we give details of these in the Additional Resources at the back of this book. Here, we will concentrate on just two of the ten: the New York Shakespeare Festival production from 1974 (directed by Edwin Sherin) and the Brian Blessed/Tony Rotherham version from 1999. (There's a fine 1984 version starring Laurence Olivier, but he's already received considerable attention in this book so we leave that interpretation alone with just this mention.)

King Lear: The Sherin and Blessed Versions

Shakespeare's play opens with a scene that can only be described as self-deposition: within just over 300 lines, Lear gives up his kingdom into the rapacious hands of his two elder daughters (Goneril and Regan) and exiles his beloved youngest daughter, Cordelia, to France. He also has time to banish his faithful servant, the Earl of Kent. At the outset, Lear says that he wishes to express his "darker purpose" (36), but he never intended it to be so dark and so profoundly anarchic in its effect. He wants, in fact, just to divide up the kingdom reasonably fairly and to do so publicly in order to:

> Shake all cares and business from our age,
> Conferring them on younger strengths while we
> Unburdened crawl toward death. (39–41)

The only prop in the scene to which he makes direct reference is a map which he will use to show to those assembled who gets which part of his kingdom. So, the setting is stripped down. However, before Lear enters there's a few moments of conversation between Gloucester and Kent, in which Gloucester reveals that he (Gloucester) has an illegitimate son (Edmund) as well as a legitimate one (Edgar) and that the former has some rights ("the whoreson must be acknowledged" [23–24], as Gloucester bluntly puts it). Shakespeare's concern in this scene, then, is manifestly with power relations in the family.

So, what do Sherin and Blessed do with such an extraordinarily dramatic scene? Sherin first. Since this is a recording of a stage production, its camera work is limited, but that doesn't seem to matter. James Earl Jones as Lear dominates the stage; he is a profoundly threatening, dangerous presence: to a degree physically decrepit but radiating power nonetheless. What comes across vividly in the New York Shakespeare Festival production are two things: first, Lear's decision to divide up his kingdom publicly according to how effusive his three daughters can be in declaring their love is

114

nothing short of child abuse; second, the reason behind Cordelia's underwhelming response—"Nothing, my lord" she says, in answer to Lear's command to "Speak" (86, 87)—is that she suffers an acute bout of what might be termed "stage fright." With her two older sisters looking on, sisters who have passed the test, she panics and tells the truth to her father:

> I love Your Majesty
> According to my bond, no more nor less. (92–93)

Sherin's direction really works beautifully at this point. It works all the better because everything else about the scene (most notably the stripped-down setting and the slate-gray costumes) serves to force the audience to focus on the drama on stage. There is only one piece of color: Cordelia's costume has bands of white slashed across the palette of gray as if to emphasize her purity. It's good that the Lear scene works, for the opening exchange between Gloucester, Kent, and Edmund is wooden and unconvincing—a weak beginning in an otherwise fine interpretation. And Lear's map, that sole prop? A large tapestry laid down on the floor, large enough for Lear to walk on to indicate how he will divide up the kingdom.

A quarter of a century later, Brian Blessed (a veteran of the British stage and screen) takes his turn; he does so, of course, with the potential knowledge of how every other director has taken on the task. It's a situation shot through with the anxiety of influence. Since Blessed's version is filmic rather than a transcription of a stage production, the interpretive possibilities are much greater. It is a low-budget production, but Blessed does have the opportunity to begin with exterior shots, and he takes advantage of the opportunity.

In this film, the medieval costumes and claustrophobic, focused rendering of 1974 have gone. They are replaced with druidic costumes and a coming together of the people around an ancient monument to hear their king. Gone, too, is Lear's physical decrepitude, for Blessed (as Lear) rides hard toward the camera at the very beginning of the film. After the brief exterior shot, the action moves to an interior setting of a cave lit with torches. It is here that the king holds court.

Blessed's reading of the role is very different from Jones's. He finds moments of humor in Lear; he shows signs of senility as he has to be prompted, at one point, to continue with a scene that he has clearly stage-managed. Perhaps the most intriguing part of the interpretation from a comparative point of view is that where Jones could barely contain his aggression, Blessed seems throughout to be toying with his people and his family. He is thoroughly enjoying being the center of attention one last time; he intends to make the most of it. When he banishes Cordelia, he seems more offended at her choosing to critique her sisters' expressions of love than anything else, for by doing so she points up how much of a sham the whole business is.

Three further points of comparison we would briefly make. First, one prop remains the same: the tapestry map. Much reduced in size and more symbolic than cartographic, the map is similarly laid out on the ground for Lear to point at as he describes his proposed division of lands. Second, the opening scene between Gloucester, Kent, and Edmund is much better handled than in the earlier production. The acting is less wooden; the sauciness of some of Gloucester's language is more clearly shown; and Edmund's sense of being offended by the whole thing comes across better. Third, Blessed's Lear is consistently and convincingly underplayed: he seems puzzled by rather than angry at Cordelia's failure to go along with his little game. It is a shame that the production values aren't better, for to his credit Blessed does have something new to say about *King Lear* even after almost a century of filmed versions of one of Shakespeare's greatest tragedies.

Analysis and Interpretation: King Lear

1. Peter Brook once commented that *King Lear* is a play that is impossible to film. What about *Lear* would make a producer and filmmaker make such a comment? What problems do you think filmmakers would encounter in trying to translate *Lear* from the stage to the screen?

2. How would you stage the first scene of *King Lear*? How would you depict the king? How would you use setting, costume, subtext to reinforce the overall interpretation? How would you

handle the transition from the opening dialogue among Gloucester, Kent, and Edmund to the court scene and public spectacle that immediately follows?

3. As we indicated earlier, there are numerous versions of *King Lear* available on DVD. Why is this tale of an aging king so popular in a culture which has turned increasingly towards youth? What is enduring about the play's message? How do particular films bring this message out?

4. The opening scene in *King Lear* is rightly famous in the Shakespeare canon. Is there another scene that is as memorable? Lear's reconciliation with Cordelia, for example, or the climax of the play and Lear's death? How has that scene you've chosen been handled by directors other than Sherin and Blessed? Does there seem to be a traditional interpretation that directors acknowledge in the way they handle the play?

Macbeth

Where *King Lear* is about paying too high a price for an initial act of breathtaking foolishness, *Macbeth* focuses on another human failing: ambition (male ambition in Macbeth's desire to be king; female ambition in Lady Macbeth's wish to see her husband's ambition fulfilled). Shakespeare is also concerned with something else, something which only surfaces in one other tragedy: *Antony and Cleopatra*. What are the dynamics within a relationship that facilitate dysfunction? Is Macbeth's oh-so-brief triumph the result of marital synergy? Would Macbeth have succeeded alone? And then there's the role of the supernatural in human affairs. Nowhere else in Shakespeare does so explicit a concern with the world beyond show up as in *Macbeth*'s three witches.

Given the popularity of Shakespeare's "Scottish play" on stage, it's surprising that there have not been more feature films made of *Macbeth*. Orson Welles' 1948 black-and-white version is a mixture of brilliant and inventive cinematography and low-budget production and editing. Welles reportedly was caught up in a dispute with the studio over the soundtrack, and the post-production work was redone without Welles' involvement. The film has been re-released with its original sound, in which the actors speak with sometimes inconsistent and distracting pseudo-Scottish accents. While it's clearly not the major achievement that Welles' *Othello* represents, this *Macbeth* is an intriguing, expressionistic rendition of the play from a powerful director. In truth, however, the meritorious cinematic versions of *Macbeth* come down to two, both of which fulfill the possibilities inherent in Welles' magnificent failure of more than 60 years ago now. One, Kurosawa's *Throne of Blood* we look at it in some detail in Chapter 5 as an example of how directors have "transformed" Shakespeare and not just adapted his work. The other we will look at now: Roman Polanski's 1971 effort. (There is also a 2006 version, directed by Geoffrey Wright and set in Melbourne's underworld; it's entertaining but too hip and ingratiating to merit discussion.)

Polanski's *Macbeth* (1971)

Polanski's version of Shakespeare's *Macbeth* was financed by *Playboy* and marketed in part using its violence and nudity as audience draws, a fact which has darkened its reputation among Shakespeare scholars ever since. This is the case even though both elements in the film fail to shock in ways they once did, and, of course, as Deborah Cartmell points out, violence is an integral part of Shakespearean theater anyway. (See her essay on violence in her *Interpreting Shakespeare on Screen.*) Despite its bad reputation (indeed, despite *Polanski's* bad reputation), the film is in fact very well made and remains vibrant more than 30 years after it was finished..

The weird sisters play an especially prominent role in the film. This prominence begins with Polanski's treatment of the play's first scene, a scene which places the witches front and center. Polanski has a hard nut to crack: how do you stage the three witches' scene convincingly when Shakespeare is staging something which many of us would say does not exist in any corporeal sense. It was easier during the early-modern period when witches were believed in as manifestations of a dangerous noumenal world that could impinge on the everyday world at any moment and with disastrous results.

118

Polanski's film opens with a long shot of a lonely beach as dawn comes up. A single seagull flies in the distance across our view. In the foreground, three ragged beings (two older women and one who is quite young) begin to scratch symbols on the moist sand. Into a hole, they place a noose, a severed arm, and a dagger. They cover these up as they fill in the hole they have just dug. One of them pours liquid on the sand, and they begin to chant. Their words are those of Shakespeare's play (all but the last half-dozen, rather obscure lines about Grimalkin and Paddock, which Polanski—perhaps wisely—chooses to cut). The quotidian subtext is that they are checking with each other when and where they will next meet. Then they move very slowly off camera into the distance, the only sound the creaking wheels of their cart on which they carried the totemic objects they have just buried. The mists come in, and the opening credits roll. It's 3 minutes and 24 seconds of brilliance: riveting; disturbing; mysterious; scary. we don't think it could have been, or has been done, better.

Analysis and Interpretation: Polanski's Macbeth

1. Compare Polanski's version of *Macbeth* with Welles' 1948 take on the play. They are obviously very different in their cinematic style and presentation. Welles' film is in black and white and uses a stylized, symbolic set; Polanski's aims for historical realism. How does this difference change the focus and impact of the story?

2. Lady Macbeth's role in Macbeth's tragedy has been one of the most interesting points of discussion among audiences. How does Polanski's sense of her role differ from that presented in any other version (the 1979 RSC version, perhaps, with Ian McKellen and Judi Dench in the leading roles, or the 1982 Bard Productions' interpretation directed by Arthur Allan Seidelman)? How are her role and influence interpreted differently by the two filmmakers?

3. The conundrum with Macbeth, the "bloody butcher," is how to make him sufficiently sympathetic to enable an audience to care. *No* sympathy surely translates to *no* interest, and that means dramatic disaster. How have some of the film versions of *Macbeth* dealt with this issue? What cinematic strategies have they used to

make Macbeth a sympathetic figure. Staging? Subtext? Camera technique?

4. *Macbeth* is one of Shakespeare's shortest plays. (There's a scholarly argument with significant support that says the text we have is a shortened touring version of a longer, lost original.) Yet, directors do like to cut (and, for that matter, to rearrange) Shakespeare's lines. How have some of the versions of *Macbeth* accomplished these tasks? What seems to be the rationale behind the film scripts? Does one rationale seem to you to be more convincing than another? Why?

CHAPTER 5

Transformations

One of the most difficult questions to deal with when it comes to cinematic treatments of Shakespeare is deciding where faithful interpretation ends and radical adaptation begins. Films of Shakespeare's plays line up rather scruffily along a continuum. Because they do so, it is not possible to provide a clear demarcation line that separates one sort of Shakespeare film from another. It is possible to say that the BBC TV versions of Shakespeare are likely to be textually accurate. It is possible to say that a film version of Shakespeare by an auteur such as Akiro Kurosawa will wander far from the original. Neither statement clarifies a definitional principle, however. Each just renders a judgment on a specific film. You could apply descriptions such as "adapted from," "based on," or "inspired by," but these, of course, simply kick the can down the road by using new phrases which need definition.

The easiest way to answer this question and, so, be able to group radical Shakespeare adaptations on film together is to look at intention. What is the purpose of the film? Does the director intend to represent Shakespeare accurately on film—always allowing for the sort of translation that goes on when art is transferred from one medium (the stage) to another (the film set)? Does the director see Shakespeare as an opportunity to go off in his or her own direction in order to create meaning that is tangential to Shakespeare's purpose? If the former, then the film (within limits) is accurate and faithful. If the latter, then the film is a radical adaptation (or transformation) and deserves to be studied on its own merits as a film. For example, if you look at Arclight Films' 2006 production of *Macbeth* (directed by Geoffrey Wright and starring Sam Worthington as Macbeth) it is fairly straightforward to categorize on the evidence of your eyes and ears. On the one hand, the fact that Wright transfers the action to the underworld of contemporary Melbourne and uses his trademark jittery camera work with gusto would suggest a significant adaptation awaits. On the other, Wright's persistent use of Shakespeare's original language indicates that his purpose is to make Shakespeare accessible rather than to go off on his own to create a film's whose meaning is separable from Shakespeare's early Jacobean original. The same argument hold, too, with Alexander Fodor's 2007 version of *Hamlet*. Fodor (as director) monkeys around with the characterization of Shakespeare's original but remains remarkably faithful to the language of the play. And then there's Welles' *Chimes at Midnight* which is authentically Shakespearean even as Welles puts together the pieces of Falstaff's life in a way Shakespeare himself never did.

It is on this category of radical filmic adaptations of Shakespeare— those which are only loosely based on Shakespeare—that this chapter will dwell so as to give you a sense of how talented directors have used Shakespeare in recent times to tell their own stories on film. It will give you a sense too of how relevant Shakespeare remains because his basic plots are so compelling and his characters three-dimensional. Who cannot be moved by love, murder, sorrow, or joy? Who can ignore personalities as vivid as Hamlet, Lear, Othello, Portia, Rosalind, or Beatrice? Who can fail to be drawn in by the magic of Prospero? You can see the original behind the transformation even as our attention will be on just how fundamental the alterations are.

To do so, we will look at several films: Kurosawa's *Ran* and *Throne of Blood*, Billy Morrissette's *Scotland, Pa.*, Tim Blake Nelson's *O*, Gil Junger's *10 Things I Hate about You*, and Andrew Fleming's *Hamlet 2*. Tragedy and comedy. we would have liked to have added Ari Karusmäki's 1987 film *Hamlet Goes Business* (*Hamlet liikemaailmassa*) to the mix to give a sense of what happens when tragedy becomes satire and Elsinore becomes a Finnish corporation, but the film is not widely enough available at this time to make our discussion useful. We also considered Kurosawa's *The Bad Sleep Well*, but variations on *Hamlet* and Kurosawa himself will be well enough represented here— and the film is not Kurosawa's best either by a long shot. And finally

Paul Mazursky's *Tempest* was tempting because it is such a fine work in its own right and because Shakespeare's romances are often overlooked. However, since few good film versions of Shakespeare's romances have *ever* been made and none is easily available (*Prospero's Books* comes to mind here) and since, for that reason, we don't have a chapter in *Screening Shakespeare* on that dramatic genre any discussion of Mazursky's drama would have lacked the necessary context.

Ran (1985)

Kurosawa's *Ran* (*Chaos* in Japanese) is the third in a series of radical adaptations of Shakespeare's tragedies. The first two were *Throne of Blood* (based on *Macbeth*) and *The Bad Sleep Well* (based on *Hamlet*). With *Ran* , he moves on to *King Lear*. How radical are Kurosawa's changes? For a start, the setting is the world of the medieval Samurai. The three daughters have, then, become the three sons of Hidetora: Taro, Jiro, and Saburo. The opening shot is not, as it would be if Kurosawa's intent were to transcribe Shakespeare's tragedy, the king dividing up his lands. Instead, Kurosawa shows us in a series of long shots a broad sweep of hillside and grasslands with several warriors on horseback scanning the horizon in different directions. After the title credits, the scene shifts to what looks like a wild-boar hunt. *King Lear* transformed this clearly is.

In addition to switching the gender of Lear's children, Kurosawa melds the characters of Edmund and Cornwall (the two most profoundly transgressive people in *King Lear's* cast) into one woman: the Lady Kaede. She symbolizes the predicament of women in a male-dominated society. And there are important differences in characterization, too. Shakespeare's King Lear is old and foolish; Kurosawa's Hidetora is a ruthless warrior. The Fool in *Lear* (who disappears half way through the action) becomes a character rather than a function in Kyoami. There's the acting style, too, with its elements of the stiff formality and otherworldliness of Noh theater. The plot differs markedly from *Lear* especially towards the end where the forces arrayed against Hidetora and the "phantasmagoric violence" (as Michael Sragow has put it) remind us of *Macbeth* more than *Lear*. Kurosawa himself always insisted that he didn't base his film on *Lear* but on tales of the warlord Mori Motonari. He only saw

123

the connections with Shakespeare's play when he was well into writing the script for the film. Be that as it may, Kurosawa's extraordinary film shows the possibilities of transforming Shakespeare into the cultural language of other countries, of moving a work away from the Western tradition.

Throne of Blood (1957)

It has been argued by Roger Manvell that Kurosowa's *Throne of Blood* (*The Castle of the Spider's Web* in Japanese) is actually a "transmutation, a distillation of the *Macbeth* theme, not an adaptation" (107). This remark is astute because what strikes any audience about the film is that there is almost no dialogue, and what dialogue there is is not, of course, Shakespeare's. So, Kurosawa has to rely in his film on cinematic techniques and (as with *Ran*) on the minimalist acting techniques derived from Noh theater. Peter Hindle in his *Studying Shakespeare on Film* does a fine job of analyzing Kurosawa's film as radical adaptation. As Hindle remarks: *Throne of Blood* is "unique in reworking Shakespeare's play for the big screen using a non-Western society's culture and history so radically that the result is unparalleled in the Shakespeare film genre" (99).

The supernatural and ritualistic elements in *Macbeth* (which begin with the initial three witches' scene in Shakespeare's play) are transformed into another idiom entirely by Kurosawa's use of a formal set design characteristic of Noh drama, by the hypnotic music with which the film begins, and by a chorus of droning male voices. The acting, too, enshrines the Noh paradox of intense emotion and physical stillness. In Kurosawa's film, one symbol comes to stand for the air of confusion and mystery that characterizes Shakespeare's last great tragedy: the Spiderweb Forest. At one level, this is a transformation of the heath on which Macbeth and Banquo meet the witches; on another, it comes to stand for the emotional confusion of Macbeth (Washizu in *Throne of Blood*), a confusion that renders him particularly vulnerable to the witches' prophecies.

In the course of the film, Kurosawa uses camera techniques brilliantly to disorient the viewer and to make Macbeth's consternation and confusion work cinematically. Gone is the first human scene in

Macbeth, where Duncan assesses the state of the battle (1.2). In its place is the Spiderweb Forest, and the indelible image of warriors astride horses that restively move from side to side as if to mirror the confusion of their riders. Washizu's response to the situation is to fire an arrow into a tree's highest branches. What else would a warrior do? The result? Only a disembodied, spine-chilling wail.

Macbeth is one of Shakespeare's most mysterious plays because it forces the audience to confront the role of the unseen in life. Kurosawa achieves the same effect on film with great deftness and without in any way slavishly imitating the Shakespearean original. It is a rare case of one master craftsman paying homage to another through artistic transformation. And the rest of the film is as fine as the opening as we see in the final scene of *Throne*: The wrecked castle dissolving into the mists and the chanting of the moral to the tale. In English, the moral reads:

> Look upon the ruins
> Of the castle of delusion
> Haunted only now
> By the spirits of those who perished
> A scene of carnage
> Born of consuming desire
> Never changing
> Now and throughout eternity.

Scotland, Pa. (2001)

Scotland, Pa. is director Billy Morrissette's take on *Macbeth*. The film has none of the brilliance of Kurosawa's transformation of Shakespearean text into film, but it is clever, allusive, and intertextual. It tries a little *too* hard and it runs out of steam towards the end, but it is well worth examining for what it says about the contemporary sensibility and its response to a literary classic that is now more than 400 years old.

Scotland, Pa. offers a series of correspondences by way of transformation, correspondences that remain just close enough to the original to allow those in the know to smile. So, the three witches at the beginning of the play become three odd types sitting, stoned, up on a Ferris wheel at a funfair late at night. The film begins with their conversation. It's worth quoting in full because it mimics so closely the moral contradiction which the witches present in the rhyming couplet at the end of Act 1, Scene 1: "Fair is foul, and foul is fair" (11).

The trio in Morrissette's film is off camera eating from a bucket of chicken and smoking joints:

Witch 1
"Light another one. [Laughter] That feels sexy."

Witch 2
"Shh! I spook easily."

Witch 3 [as we see an unidentifiable container fall to the the ground]
"Oh, Christ! Who dropped the chicken? I would have eaten that!"

Witch 2
"No. It was foul. The fowl was foul."

Witch 1
"And the fair was fair."

Witch 2
"The foul was fair."

Witch 3
"The fair is foul."

Witch 2
"My ass hurts."

Witch 3
"I don't think that one works."
[Pause]

Witch 3
"Shh! She's having a spell."

Witch 2
"Oh god! She's so dramatic!"

And there are other references to the witches. One of the opening threesome shows up twice more as a fortune teller—although it's likely she and the other witches are merely imagined by the central character, one Joe ("Mac") McBeth, a cook at the local greasy spoon called *Duncan's*. His wife, Pat, is learning to use the ice-cream machine, and just before she finally does she mutters: "Let's hope thirteen's a charm." And just in case we don't get the point, there's a reference to something like the First Witch's incantation: "And like a rat without a tail / I'll do, I'll do, and I'll do" (1.3.9–10). This time through, though, it's bathetic: a customer gets angry and shouts: "I don't give a rat's ass!"

In fact, the strength of this re-visioning of *Macbeth* is that everything is reduced to tawdriness. Instead of becoming Thane of Cawdor, Mac is promoted to assistant manager of *Duncan's*. Instead of being stabbed to death, the restaurant's owner, Norm Duncan, is drowned in a deep-fat fryer. Instead of vying for the crown, the modern-day McBeths are lesser mortals indeed. Banquo's feast becomes a game of Yahtzee at the local bar. Macduff becomes a marginally competent police detective. Macbeth's famous soliloquy about the meaninglessness of existence ("Tomorrow, and tomorrow, and tomorrow" [5.4.19]) is reduced to banal self-help tapes playing on the tape deck in the detective's car: "Tomorrow is tomorrow. Tomorrow is not today." As Pat McBeth puts it to her husband in the film's best line: "We're not bad people, Mac. We're just underachievers who have to make up for lost time."

The list of allusions to *Macbeth* continues throughout the film, and as if one play weren't enough, Morrissette slyly offers echoes of several other Shakespeare plays: *Antony and Cleopatra, Hamlet, Richard III, The Tempest*. He even manages a nod to *Citizen Kane*. Along the way he also pokes fun at modern-day fast-food outlets (the owner of *Duncan's* loves donuts; after his murder the McBeths take over the restaurant, add a drive thru, and rechristen it *McBeth's*). In fact, Morrissette's target is, we suspect, really small-town rural America with its preoccupation with guns, for they feature prominently throughout the plot.

The film itself is more than competent from a technical point of view, and employs a consistently muted palette of yellows and greens with most of the scenes appropriately shot at night. It's as if Morrissette can't make up his mind whether to make a serious indie film or just to sit back and show how much Shakespeare he can pack into 104 minutes. In the end, the Shakespearean pastiche wins out: Joe McBeth dies impaled by McDuff on the steer horns attached to the hood of his car; Pat McBeth, driven crazy by a burn she got when Norm Duncan was drowned in the deep-fat fryer, hacks off her hand as a grisly solution to the original Lady Macbeth's preoccupation with the blood on her hands after the murder of the king. This film is genuinely interesting and revelatory of the contemporary sensibility even as it ultimately disappoints.

O (2001)

O is a more serious film than *Scotland, Pa.* It alludes repeatedly to its source, *Othello*, in the naming of its characters, in the basics of its plot, in its emphasis on violence. It works as an indictment of teen violence and the whole drug culture, but it seems at times to be rather melodramatic and preachy.

The plot involves the same basic relationships as those in *Othello*, but the setting has been transported to a contemporary high-school setting and to the realm of sports. So, the protagonist Odin (Othello) excels in basketball rather than war, for example, and the preoccupation is with drugs rather than with witchcraft. As in *Othello*, the ending is tragic, so the trio of Odin, Desi, and Hugo (Othello, Desdemona, and Iago) end up with their lives utterly wasted beyond the possibility of redemption.. Out of jealousy, Odin kills Desi in a rage brought on by drugs; Odin commits suicide after he realizes how he has been tricked; and Hugo (in the film's final scene) is taken away in a police car. In a voice-over, he chillingly predicts he will have his 15 minutes of fame.

This film was not very successful at the box office earning some $16,000,000 in first run. It may be that its connection with *Othello* carried too much gravitas for a teen movie. It is more likely that historical coincidence played a bigger role. The film was finished in

1999, but its completion occurred at the time of the Columbine High School shootings, so its release was postponed. The potential audience may simply not have wanted to see reality, but something distanced from it. There may have been some reaction too against its content: drugs; gun violence; and one nasty sex scene that is really an act of rape.

10 Things I Hate about You (1999)

In his recent *Shakespeare and Film*, Samuel Crowl comments on Gil Junger's *10 Things* as an example (one among several) of recent films which have "employed Shakespeare as an essential component of the narrative" (18). He goes on to emphasize the film's setting, and to put it in the company of *Tromeo and Juliet*, *O,* and *Shakespeare in Love*. In some ways, Crowl's observation is odd: Isn't it precisely the distance from Shakespeare that distinguishes films such as Junger's from more faithful adaptations? And if that's true, then what "essence" is being referred to? And if this "essence" is only a "component," is it in fact "essential." One of the tag lines used in advertising the film suggests it isn't essential: "How do I loathe thee? Let me count the ways." That, after all, is perhaps the most famous line from Elizabeth Barrett Browning's *Sonnets from the Portuguese*. Not Shakespeare, then.

Again and again, reviewers and film scholars point out that *10 Things* updates *The Taming of the Shrew*, one of Shakespeare's earliest (and these days most controversial) comedies. Yet, the cast list suggests more a piecemeal plundering of the Shakespeare canon (a sort of allusiveness on the cheap) than anything else: Shakespeare himself and *Othello* are alluded to with "Bianca Stratford"—as much as *Taming*. The late Heath Ledger's character "Patrick Verona" suggests *Romeo and Juliet* or *Two Gentlemen of Verona* rather than *Taming* (which takes place in Padua). Only Julia Stiles' "Kat Stratford" echoes *Taming*'s Kate. As Roger Ebert put it in his review of the film: it is "is inspired, in a sortuva kinduva way, by Shakespeare's *The Taming of the Shrew*, in the same sense that *Starship Troopers'* was inspired by *Titus Andronicus*. It doesn't remake Shakespeare so much as evoke him as a talisman. . . ."

Nor should the allusiveness to Shakespeare (not his essence so much as his bones) hide the cookie-cutter quality of the plot. How many teen films have there been the plots of which turn on a contrast between siblings (or friends), one of whom is popular and one of whom is loathed, or one of whom is not too bright and one of whom is brainy? Add to that the key device of a bribe beings offered to take the latter girl out, and the number is legion. Add the setting (the high-school prom), and the number becomes stratospheric. Perhaps the most intriguing part of the film's narrative is Patrick Verona's being offered $300 to take Kat Stratford out to the prom. Echoes of Shylock and his 3000 ducats? Now *that* allusion (if it is one) genuinely reverberates.

That said, the film is very entertaining. The opening sequence is funny because its relentless evisceration of high-school's cliques is so accurate, but the pulsating overlaid credits (in, predominantly, a nauseating shade of green) shout out that this is a teen flick and should be taken at face value and not for what it reveals about Shakespeare's art. It is well acted; it is well directed as far as pacing is concerned; the music helps to pass the time enjoyably. However, as a transformation of Shakespeare, *10 Things* does not stand scrutiny. Shakespeare and Junger pass on parallel tracks going in opposite directions: Shakespeare towards a serious discussion of women's role in marriage; Junger towards laughs for the sake of laughs. The school counselor (humorously called Ms. Perky) is a closet romance writer, and when we are allowed a glimpse at the first line of her latest potboiler on her laptop's screen we know we're in for a long 97 minutes. The line reads: "As his hand slid up her creamy white thighs, she could feel his huge member pulsating with desire." And that line is then followed by a truly pointless joke about a bratwurst (which, of course, Ms. Perky incorporates into her magnum opus).

Perhaps the film might have worked better if those responsible (Junger, and Karen McCullah Lutz and Kirsten Smith as co-writers) had worked out some way in which to include the Christopher Sly Induction—always the most interesting (because metadramatic) element in the original play. we would have thought it more interesting as a "transformation" of Shakespeare (although "glancing homage" might be a better—if oxymoronic—term for what the film tries to do) if we had not felt that its acquaintance with *Taming* were not a shrewd, even cynical, effort to appeal to an older demographic. When it comes to getting people to go to movie houses, it's well to split your bets.

Hamlet 2 (2008)

If Gil Junger's strategy was to mine Shakespeare for allusions and layer on top a teen comedy from off one of the lower shelves, Andrew Fleming's is to employ parody and the motif of the play-within-the-play (so beloved of Shakespeare) to provide some energy for his narrative. Along the way, his film skewers an entire sub-genre of feel-good teaching movies: most directly (because all three are mentioned in *Hamlet 2*) *Dead Poets' Society*, *Dangerous Minds*, and *Mr. Holland's Opus*. The basic storyline of the film (a storyline which actually owes more to those Judy Garland—Mickey Rooney musicals of the 1930s than anything else) involves a bad actor and worse high-school drama teacher deciding to stage a musical sequel to *Hamlet* in a desperate effort to save himself and also his school's drama department from closing because of budget cuts.

The musical sequel has definite possibilities (at least it's rather creative) as Prince Hamlet and Jesus (yes, *that* Jesus) use a time machine to try to rescue Gertrude (from drinking the poison) and Ophelia (from drowning herself). However, the film's tagline suggests broad laughs will be the order of the day: "One high school drama teacher is about to make a huge number 2."

However, such a suggestion actually turns out not to be the case. Yes, there are stupid jokes such as the fertility clinic named the "Prickly Pear." Yet, there's a lot of sharp social commentary too that bears some relation to Shakespearean wit. The setting is Tucson, and the writers (Pam Brady and Andrew Fleming) take dead aim at urban blight with their glance at a run-down motel called the "Americana." The setting is also, of course, more narrowly a high school, and the teacher's response to one of his student's comments is cringingly good. The drama teacher (Mr. Marschz, played by Steve Coogan) says "Thanks for the truth sandwich, my little brother." Take that for the false camaraderie that characterizes high school. And there are funny one liners delivered with mordant wit by Catherine Keener. To her boring boarder (yes, the pun is meant), she says: "They should just ship you on over to the Gulf. You know, let you talk to people. All the terrorists would just kill themselves."

What has all this to do with Shakespeare? Well, there's the dependence of the sequel on the original: *Hamlet* 2 on, yes, *Hamlet* 1. There's the featured role of Laertes, who now has new dialogue (including the deathless line: "Oh, I'm going to kick destiny in the butt!!!!!!!"). There's the reference to Hamlet's ghost as symbolic of the restraining patriarchal figure we "all" encounter in our lives. There's the division of the action into five Acts with a voice-over (done by Peter O'Toole) akin to the Chorus in *Henry V*. There's the humorous (sort of) reference to Bottom in *Midsummer Night's Dream*. Above all, there's the admission that Shakespeare can't be topped but only learned from. So, the student drama-critic (one Noah Sapperstein) remarks about "Hamlet 2" (the musical-within-the-film): "Sometimes an idea can be so bad, it starts to turn good again." And so, Mr. Marschz opines to one of his students' parents: "I just wondered why in *Hamlet* everybody has to die. It's such a downer! I mean, if Hamlet had had just a little bit of therapy he could have turned everything around. Everybody deserves a second chance."

What we have with *Hamlet* 2, which we don't get with, for example *10 Things I Hate about You*, is genuine transformation of the source text. The film is slow and at times dull, but it's also a clever parody of contemporary society and its preoccupations. In that way, it's more indebted to *Merry Wives of Windsor* or to Ben Jonson's drama of social satire than it is to *Hamlet*. As you would expect of a transformation, in this case a film does more than make knowing allusions to the greatest name in the Western tradition.

Analysis and Interpretation: Transformations

1. How effective is any one of the adaptations discussed in this chapter in its use of the original source. Does the film merit being watched in its own right? Why or why not?

2. Received opinion has it that Kurosawa's two films, *Ran* and *Throne of Blood* are masterpieces and the other examples discussed in this chapter are comparative second raters. How fair is such a judgment? Which of the films discussed as adaptations resonates most for you? Why?

3. One of the supposed values of these transformations is that they are sufficiently removed from their Shakespearean originals to be appreciated without reference to the plays to which they bear a distant relation. Is that true? Does it matter if a viewer of one of these films has no background in Shakespeare? Does he or she need that intertextual knowledge? Looked at another way: Is that Shakespearean knowledge actually a hindrance to the appreciation of films which are radical adaptations? Why or why not?

4. Take one of Shakespeare's plays of which you are particularly fond, one which has not been the subject of discussion in this chapter. How would you transform it into a successful film in its own right? A sequel perhaps? Obviously this is a broad question, so you can only sketch out an answer in terms of what your aims or strategies would be.

5. What does it say about Shakespeare that films are constantly alluding to his work? Does it reveal more about our culture or about the background of those who create films for us? What does it say about the audience who go to films? If that audience has changed, how may that influence future cinematic treatments of Shakespeare's work?

ADDITIONAL RESOURCES

Shakespeare's Life and Works

Dobson, Michael, and Stanley Wells, ed. *The Oxford Companion to Shakespeare.* 2nd ed. Oxford: Oxford UP, 2009.

> Discusses Shakespeare's life, his experience as a playwright, actor, and businessman, his work as interpreted on film, and his international reputation. Good coverage of current scholarship. Excellent black-and-white drawings and photos of key performers and performances.

Dunton-Downer, Leslie, and Alan Riding. *Essential Shakespeare Handbook.* New York: DK Publishing, 2004.

> The most accessible and best illustrated guide in a crowded field. Covers all of Shakespeare's plays and poems; it begins with a brief survey of his life, Elizabethan culture, and the important historical moments of the period. Intended for a general audience.

Kastan, David Scott, ed. *A Companion to Shakespeare.* Oxford: Blackwell, 1999.

> A very helpful, authoritative guide to Shakespeare's socio-cultural background. Particularly useful for coverage of issues that are too often ignored: reading practices in Elizabethan England, the status of writing in the period, the traditions of acting during Shakespeare's life, and the printing business at the turn of the seventeenth century. Twenty-nine essays by experts in Shakespeare studies. Would benefit from more illustrations.

Laroque, François. *The Age of Shakespeare*. Trans. Alexandra
    Campbell. New York: Harry N. Abrams, 1993.

> A pocket-sized book for general readers, *The Age of
> Shakespeare* includes an impressive collection of images, many
> of which are in color. Typical period dress, architecture, and
> daily life as well as famous paintings and historical documents
> are presented in this readable and engaging book. Includes
> biographical information on and images of Shakespeare, a
> discussion of the mythology of Queen Elizabeth, and a
> chapter on the changes occurring after the queen's death and
> the accession to the throne of the first of the Stuart
> monarchs, James I. A good source for historical background
> on England and Europe during the period.

Pritchard, R. E. *Shakespeare's England: Life in Elizabethan & Jacobean
    Times*. Charleston, SC: The History P, 2003.

> An entertaining and surprisingly insightful collection of
> excerpts by and about those living in Elizabethan England.
> Sections on "Women and Men," "London," and "Poverty,
> Crime and Punishment" among others. Sometimes tries
> almost too hard to appeal to the reader; however, the section
> introductions are helpful.

Schoenbaum, S. *Shakespeare: The Globe & the World*. New York:
    Folger Shakespeare Library/Oxford UP, 1979.

> A little dated now, but this heavily illustrated guide to
> Shakespeare and his culture remains indispensible.
> Schoenbaum can always be relied upon for the accuracy of
> his observations.

Wells, Stanley, and Lena Cowen Olin, ed. *Shakespeare*. An Oxford
    Guide. New York: Oxford UP, 2003.

> A dense collection of essays by experts in the field. Consists
> of 45 separate essays divided into four sections:
> Shakespeare's life and times, Shakespearean genres, criticism
> on Shakespeare, and "Shakespeare's Afterlife." Includes a
> very helpful general essay by Tony Howard on "Shakespeare
> on Film and Video."

Internet Resources

Film as the New Shakespeare: Reversing the Shakespeare / Film Trajectory.
http://www.ahds.ac.uk/performingarts/collections/film-as-new-shakespeare.htm

Housed at the University of Glasgow, this site was last updated in 2007. It has some merits, but it is not as "Shakespeare-centric" as its title suggests.

In Search of Shakespeare: Shakespeare on Film—Professional Development.
www.pbs.org/shakespeare/educators/film/ lessonplan.html

A Web site with a number of worthwhile pedagogical links. More directed at instructors than students. Some of its advice is too basic. It was last updated in 2003.

The Internet Movie Database. www.imdb.com

A comprehensive guide to films and the film industry. Includes a useful advanced search function as well as simple searches by title, author, director, or actor. Provides complete cast and crew credits for all of the films discussed in *Screening Shakespeare* as well as links to professional and user reviews. There are English and German versions of this site, and there's also a more extensive fee-based version: www.imdbpro.com.

Movie Review Query Engine. www.mrqe.com

A search engine useful for finding reviews of specific films. Includes reviews of early as well as recent Shakespeare films, many contemporary with a film's release. Also includes reviews of DVD re-releases. It includes almost 75,000 titles in its database and 750,000 reviews.

Shakespeare on Screen. www.folger.edu/html/folger_institute/visual/sh_pathfinder.htm

A useful Web site divided into 11 sections. Its major weakness is that it hasn't been updated since 1999.

General Film Resources

Bordwell, David, and Kristin Thompson. *Film Art: An Introduction*, 8th ed. New York: McGraw-Hill, 2008.

> Bordwell and Thompson's readable textbook remains the most popular for college film-courses. It is widely available in campus bookstores. The standard text in film analysis and history, *Film Art* includes six sections (production, form, genre, style, analyses, and history) and a glossary. It also comes with a CD of video clips.

Buckland, Warren. *Teach Yourself Film Studies*. 3rd ed. New York: McGraw Hill, 2008.

> Exactly what it says it is with an emphasis on contemporary films. It's weakest in its coverage of theory.

Giannetti, Louis. *Understanding Movies*. 11th ed. Englewood Cliffs, NJ: Prentice-Hall, 2007.

> Covers all the major concepts in film: acting, casting, cintematography, editing, mise en scene, movement, sound, storyboarding, screenwriting, and theory. Giannetti's book is well illustrated and uses a wide range of examples. His extensive discussion of *Citizen Kane* is well informed but hardly original.

Hayward, Susan. *Key Concepts in Cinema Studies*. 3rd ed. New York: Routledge, 2006.

> A very detailed, substantial, and comprehensive discussion of film concepts. More than 500 pages in length and organized alphabetically. Three useful indexes: Film, Name, and Subject. The first runs from *A bout de soufflé* to *Zulu Love Letter*.

Hill, John, and Pamela Church Gibson, ed. *The Oxford Guide to Film Studies*. Oxford: Oxford UP, 1998.

> A collection of essays on theory, concepts, methods, and issues. Useful because of the different points of view

represented by the numerous contributors, it would nevertheless benefit from greater overall coherence.

Metz, Christian. *Film Language: A Semiotics of the Cinema*. 1974. Chicago: The U of Chicago P, 1991.

Some of the discussion seems a little dated now (it was first published in French in 1968), but Metz's discussion of realism, montage, and modernity remains very important for understanding film's effects.

Nelmes, Jill, ed. *An Introduction to Film Studies*. 4th ed. London: Routledge, 2007.

This text offers a more theoretical take on film studies than Bordwell and Thompson do. Includes very interesting chapters on the film industry and film technology, and a good if challenging introduction to contemporary feminist and psychoanalytic film theories. Has a particularly fine chapter on "Ethnicity, Race and Cinema." Very well illustrated.

Shakespeare and Film

Buchanan, Judith. *Shakespeare on Film*. London: Longman, 2005.

Covers the history of Shakespeare on film from the silent era to recent developments. Buchanan's particular interest is in the relation between Shakespeare and the wider cultural context.

Cartmell, Deborah. *Interpreting Shakespeare on Screen*. New York: St. Martin's, 2000.

Cartmell's study is intended for college readers and takes a critical approach, looking at key issues in specific plays. Chapter 1 considers violence in *Macbeth* and *King Lear*; Chapter 2, gender in *Hamlet*; Chapter 3, sexuality in *Romeo and Juliet* and *Much Ado About Nothing*; Chapter 4, race in *Othello* and *The Tempest*; and Chapter 5, nationalism in *Henry V*. This book offers an important application of recent critical theory to the films and a strong argument for reading Shakespeare against the grain.

Crowl, Samuel. *Shakespeare and Film. A Norton Guide.* New York: W. W. Norton, 2008.

An excellent encompassing study of Shakespeare and film. There is little that gets by Crowl as he looks at the history of Shakespeare on film (5 chapters) and the film techniques available to directors (5 chapters). The principal weakness is that he gives the director too much credit for the final product and sees Shakespeare on film as the equal of stage performance. In the first case, he undervalues collaboration; in the latter case, he undervalues presence over absence.

Davies, Anthony, and Stanley Wells, ed. *Shakespeare and the Moving Image: The Plays on Film and Television.* Cambridge: Cambridge UP, 1994.

This volume gathers 14 academic essays on various topics related to the film and television versions of major plays. It provides especially good coverage of the tragedies (at least those filmed before 1994) and includes a selective filmography.

Henderson, Diane E., ed. *A Concise Companion to Shakespeare on Screen.* Malden, MA: Blackwell, 2006.

Henderson includes 11 chapters in her edited volume. The chapters cover what you would expect (gender studies, cultural studies, historicity, the relation between film and stage, and so on). The most provocative is Elsie Walker's opening salvo: "Getting Back to Shakespeare: Whose Film Is It Anyway?"

Hindle, Maurice. *Studying Shakespeare on Film.* New York: Palgrave Macmillan, 2007.

Hindle organizes his broad subject into five sections: film terminology; the history of Shakespeare on film; genre and film; critical essays on individual films; and Shakespeare on television. Our greatest complaint is that the essay section looks at the standard array of films and misses the opportunity to go for some outré or exotic selections. The listing of his own website sounds a little self-serving.

Jackson, Russell, ed. *The Cambridge Companion to Shakespeare on Film.* 2nd ed. Cambridge: Cambridge UP, 2007.

An interesting collection of 17 original essays on various aspects of Shakespeare film. The editor, Russell Jackson, has served as consultant to Kenneth Branagh and comments effectively on some of the key issues involved in translating the plays into film. Includes essays in four areas: adaptation, genre, directors, and critical issues (among them gender, race, and nationalism). This is a fairly academic collection but useful for students and general readers who want to tackle some sophisticated approaches to the plays on film.

Jorgens, Jack J. *Shakespeare on Film.* Bloomington: Indiana UP, 1977. Lanham, MD: UP of America, 1991.

The first book-length critical survey of Shakespeare films, and still one of the most useful introductions to the serious study of the films. Includes a valuable essay on "Shakespeare and Nonverbal Expression" and detailed analyses of 16 films, focusing on the work of Welles, Polanski, Peter Brook, Franco Zeffirelli, Akira Kurosawa, and Russian director Grigori Kosintzev.

Rothwell, Kenneth S. *A History of Shakespeare on Screen: A Century of Film and Television.* 2nd ed. Cambridge: Cambridge UP, 2004.

This book is a definitive history of Shakespeare in film and television. Rothwell generously narrates the evolution of Shakespearean cinema and, so, provides context and background for individual plays. He includes a substantial if not exhaustive filmography as well. Sometimes his analysis of particular films slips into evaluation and critique, and at these points Rothwell can be both entertaining and provocative. First published in 1999, the book now covers developments up to 2003. Rothwell includes a discussion of Almereyda's *Hamlet* and Morrissette's *Scotland, Pa.*

Welsh, James M., Richard Vela, and John C. Tibbetts, ed. *Shakespeare into Film*. New York: Checkmark Books, 2002.

> This useful book combines a number of longish essays originally published in *Literature/Film Quarterly* with an encyclopedic compilation of alphabetical entries on each of the plays. This is a good starting point for any serious research project on Shakespeare and film since it includes a history of both film and film criticism.

Select Filmography

This filmography includes feature films and adaptations of Shakespeare's plays. It is limited to films currently available on DVD. With a few exceptions, it does not include films made for television or films in languages other than English. we have rarely cited the BBC made-for-TV versions of the plays. They are very accurate renditions, but are generally uninspired as films. The entire Shakespeare canon was produced by the BBC between 1978 and 1985. The DVDs are distributed in the United States by Time-Life.

Entries are alphabetical by title. When more than one film is listed for a given play, the films are listed chronologically from latest to earliest. Adaptations are listed by their titles rather than beneath the plays on which they are based.

If you are looking for additional films, or a more inclusive list of television or foreign films, we recommend searching the *Internet Movie Database*. Rothwell's *A History of Shakespeare on Screen* also includes a comprehensive filmography.

As You Like It

Kenneth Branagh, director. Brian Blessed (Duke Senior/Duke Frederick), Bryce Dallas Howard (Rosalind), Alfred Molina (Touchstone), Kevin Kline (Jaques). BBC Films, 2006

Paul Czinner, director. Laurence Olivier (Orlando), Elisabeth Bergner (Rosalind). (Black & White). Inter-Allied, 1936

The Bad Sleep Well (Warui yatsu hodo yoku nemuru')

Based on *Hamlet*. Akira Kurosawa, director. Torisho Mifune (Koichi Nishi), Takashi Shimura (Administrative Officer Moriyama), Koji Nambara (Prosecutor Horiuchi), Takeshi Katô (Itakura). Kurosawa Production Company, 1960

Chimes at Midnight

Based on Shakespeare's *Henry IV, Part 1* and *Part 2* as well as *Henry V*. Orson Welles, director. Orson Welles (Falstaff), Jeanne Moreau (Doll Tearsheet), Margaret Rutherford (Mistress Quickly), John Gielgud (Henry IV). Alpine Films, Internacional Films, 1965

Hamlet

Alexander Fodor, director. William Belchambers (Hamlet), James Frail (The Ghost), Alan Hanson (Claudius), Tallulah Sheffield (Ophelia). (Alternative title: *Fodor's Hamlet*) Zed Resistor Company, 2007

Michael Almereyda, director. Ethan Hawke (Hamlet), Kyle MacLachlan (Claudius), Diane Venora (Gertrude), Julia Stiles (Ophelia). double A Films, 2000

Kenneth Branagh, director. Kenneth Branagh (Hamlet), Derek Jacobi (Claudius), Julie Christie (Gertrude), Kate Winslet (Ophelia). Castle Rock Entertainment, 1996

Franco Zeffirelli, director. Mel Gibson (Hamlet), Alan Bates (Claudius), Glenn Close (Gertrude), Helena Bonham Carter (Ophelia). Canal +, 1991

Tony Richardson, director. Nicol Williamson (Hamlet), Anthony Hopkins (Claudius), Judy Parfitt (Gertrude), Marianne Faithfull (Ophelia). Filmway Pictures, 1969. (Unavailable on DVD)

Laurence Olivier, director. Laurence Olivier (Hamlet), Basil Sydney (Claudius), Eileen Herlie (Gertrude), Jean Simmons (Ophelia). (Black & White). Two Cities Films, 1948

Hamlet Goes Business (Hamlet liikemaailmassa)

Based on *Hamlet*. Ari Karusmäki, director. Pirkka-Pekka Petelius (Hamlet), Esko Salminen (Klaus), Kati Outinen (Ofelia), Elina Salo (Gertrude), Esko Nikkari (Polonius) (Finnish with English subtitles). Villealfa Filmproduction Oy, 1987

Hamlet 2

Based on *Hamlet*. Andrew Fleming, director. Steve Coogan (Dana Marschz), Catherine Keener (Brie Marschz), Skylar Astin (Rand Posin), Melonie Diaz (Ivonne). Bona Fide Productions, 2008

Henry V

Kenneth Branagh, director. Kenneth Branagh (King Henry V), Derek Jacobi (Chorus), Emma Thompson (Katharine). BBC, 1989

Laurence Olivier, director. Laurence Olivier (King Henry V), Leslie Banks (Chorus), Renée Asheron (Katharine). BBC, 1944

Julius Caesar

Stuart Burge, director. Charlton Heston (Antony), Jason Robards (Brutus), Richard Johnson (Cassius). Commonwealth United Entertainment, 1970

Joseph L. Mankiewicz, director. Marlon Brando (Antony), James Mason (Brutus), John Gielgud (Cassius). (Black & White). MGM, 1953

143

Brian Blessed, Tony Rotherham, directors. Brian Blessed (King Lear), Hildegarde Neil (The Fool), Phillipa Peak (Cordelia), Caroline Lennon (Goneril). Cromwell Productions, 1999

Richard Eyre, director. Ian Holm (King Lear), Timothy West (Gloucester), Barbara Flynn (Goneril), Victoria Hamilton (Cordelia). (Made for TV as part of "Performance" series). BBC, 1994

Michael Elliott, director. Laurence Olivier (King Lear), Robert Lindsay (Edmund), Leo McKern (Gloucester), Anna Calder-Marshall (Cordelia). (Made for TV). Granada Television, 1984

Alan Cooke, director. Mike Kellin (King Lear), Gela Jacobson, Melora Marshall, Kitty Winn. (Made for TV). 1982

Jonathan Miller, director. Michael Hordern (King Lear), Gillian Barge (Goneril), Penelope Wilton (Regan), Brenda Blethyn (Cordelia) (Made for TV). BBC/Time-Life, 1982

Tony Davenall, producer. Patrick Magee (King Lear), Beth Harris (Goneril), Ann Lynn (Regan), Wendy Alnut (Cordelia). (Made for TV). Thames Television, 1974

Edwin Sherin, director. James Earl Jones (King Lear), Raul Julia (Edmund), Paul Sorvino (Gloucester), Lee Chamberlin (Cordelia). (Made for TV). New York Shakespeare Festival, 1974

Ernest C. Warde, director. Frederick Warde (King Lear), Ina Hammer (Goneril), Edith Diestel (Regan), Lorraine Huling (Cordelia). Thanhouser Film Corporation, 1916.

Korol Lir

Russian version of *King Lear.* Grigori Kozintsev and Iosif Shapiro, directors. Jüri Järvet (King Lear), Elza Radzina (Goneril), Galina Volchek (Regan), Valentina Shendrikova (Cordelia). Lenfilm Studio, 1971

Love's Labour's Lost

Kenneth Branagh, director. Kenneth Branagh (Berowne), Alicia Silverstone (The Princess of France), Nathan Lane (Costard). Arts Council of England, 2000

Macbeth

Geoffrey Wright, director. Sam Worthington (Macbeth), Victoria Hill (Lady Macbeth), Steve Bastoni (Banquo). Arclight Films, 2006

Trevor Nunn, director. Ian McKellen (Macbeth), Judi Dench (Lady Macbeth), Griffith Jones (Duncan). (Made for TV). Royal Shakespeare Company, 1979

Roman Polanski, director. Jon Finch (Macbeth), Francesca Annis (Lady Macbeth), Martin Shaw (Banquo). Caliban Films, 1971

Orson Welles, director. Orson Welles (Macbeth), Jeanette Nolan (Lady Macbeth), Edgar Barrier (Banquo). (Black & White). Mercury Productions, 1948

The Merchant of Venice

Michael Radford, director. Al Pacino (Shylock), Jeremy Irons (Antonio), Joseph Fiennes (Bassanio). Spice Factory, 2004

Trevor Nunn, director. Henry Goodman (Shylock), David Bamber (Antonio), Alexander Hanson (Bassanio). The Performance Company, 2001

Jack Gold, director. Warren Mitchell (Shylock), Gemma Jones (Portia), John Nettles (Bassanio). (Made for TV). BBC/Time-Life, 1980

Jonathan Miller, director. Laurence Olivier (Shylock), Joan Plowright (Portia), Jeremy Brett (Bassanio). ITC, 1973

A Midsummer Night's Dream

Michael Hoffman, director. Kevin Kline (Bottom), Michelle Pfeiffer (Titania), Stanley Tucci (Puck). Fox Searchlight Pictures, 1999

Adrian Noble, director. Lindsay Duncan (Hippolyta /Titania), Alex Jennings (Theseus/Oberon). Arts Council of England, 1996

William Dieterle and Max Reinhardt, directors. James Cagney (Bottom), Mickey Rooney (Puck). (Black & White). Warner Bros., 1935

Much Ado about Nothing

Kenneth Branagh, director. Kenneth Branagh (Benedick), Emma Thompson (Beatrice), Denzel Washington (Don Pedro), Keanu Reeves (Don John). BBC, 1993

O

Based on *Othello*. Tim Blake Nelson, director. Mekhi Phifer (Odin James), Josh Hartnett (Hugo Goulding), Andrew Keegan (Michael Cassio), Julia Stiles (Desi Brable). Chickie the Cop, 2001

Othello

Oliver Parker, director. Laurence Fishburne (Othello), Kenneth Branagh (Iago), Irène Jacob (Desdemona), Nathaniel Parker (Cassio). Castle Rock Entertainment, 1995

Stuart Burge, director. Laurence Olivier (Othello), Maggie Smith (Desdemona), Frank Finlay (Iago), Derek Jacobi (Cassio). BHE Films, 1965

Orson Welles, director. Orson Welles (Othello), Micheál MacLiammóir (Iago), Robert Coote (Roderigo), Suzanne Cloutier (Desdemona). (Black & White). Mercury Productions, 1952

Prospero's Books

Based on *The Tempest*. Peter Greenaway, director. John Gielgud (Prospero), Michael Clark (Caliban), Isabelle Pasco (Miranda). Allied Artists Classics, 1991

Ran

Based on *King Lear*. Akira Kurosawa, director. Tatsuya Nakadai (Hidetora/Lear), Mieko Harada (Lady Kaede). (Japanese with English subtitles). Greenwich Film Productions, 1985

Richard III

Richard Loncraine, director. Ian McKellen (Richard III), Annette Bening (Queen Elizabeth), Kristin Scott Thomas (Lady Anne), Nigel Hawthorne (Duke of Clarence). Bayly/Paré Productions, 1995

Laurence Olivier, director. Laurence Olivier (Richard III), John Gielgud (Duke of Clarence), Claire Bloom (Lady Anne). L.O.P., 1955

Romeo and Juliet

Franco Zeffirelli, director. Leonard Whiting (Romeo), Olivia Hussey (Juliet), John McEnery (Mercutio). BHE Films, 1968

Scotland, Pa.

Based on *Macbeth*. Billy Morrisette, director. James LeGros (Joe "Mac" McBeth), Maura Tierney (Pat McBeth), Christopher Walken (Lieutenant McDuff). Abandon Pictures, 2001

The Taming of the Shrew

Kirk Browning, director. Fredi Olster (Katharina), March Singer (Petruchio), Stephen Schnetzer (Lucentio). (Made for TV). 1976. (Unavailable on DVD)

Franco Zeffirelli, director. Richard Burton (Petruchio), Elizabeth Taylor (Katharina). F.A.I., 1967

Sam Taylor, director. Mary Pickford (Katharina), Douglas Fairbanks (Petruchio). (Black & White). Elton Corporation, 1929

Tempest

Based on *The Tempest*. Paul Mazursky, director. John Cassavetes (Phillip), Gena Rowlands (Antonia), Raul Julia (Kalibanos), Molly Ringwald (Miranda). Columbia Pictures, 1982

The Tempest

Derek Jarman, director. Heathcote Williams (Prospero), Toyah Wilcox (Miranda), Jack Birkett (Caliban). Boyd's Company, 1979

10 Things I Hate about You

Based on *The Taming of the Shrew*. Gil Junger, director. Heath Ledger (Patrick Verona), Julia Stiles (Katarina Stratford). Touchstone Pictures, 1999

Throne of Blood (Kumonosu jô)

Based on *Macbeth*. Akira Kurosawa, director. Toshirô Mifune (Washizu/Macbeth), Isuzu Yamada (Lady Washizu). (Black & White; Japanese with English subtitles). Toho Company, 1957

Titus

Based on *Titus Andronicus*. Julie Taymor, director. Anthony Hopkins (Titus Andronicus), Jessica Lange (Tamora), Alan Cumming (Saturninus). Clear Blue Sky Productions, 1999

Tromeo and Juliet

Lloyd Kaufman, director. Jane Jensen (Juliet), Will Keenan (Romeo Que), Sean Gunn (Sammy Capulet), Flip Brown (Father Lawrence). Troma Entertainment, 1996

Twelfth Night; Or, What You Will

Trevor Nunn, director. Helena Bonham Carter (Olivia), Nigel Hawthorne (Malvolio), Imogen Stubbs (Viola). BBC Films, 1996

William Shakespeare's Romeo + Juliet

Baz Luhrmann, director. Leonardo DiCaprio (Romeo), Claire Danes (Juliet), Harold Perrineau Jr. (Mercutio). Bazmark Films, 1996

Projects for Writing and Research

The purpose of this section is to offer students a list of suggested topics for writing and research. These are meant to supplement the more focused questions that appear frequently in the earlier sections of this book under the label of "Analysis and Interpretation."

Focus on Directors. Choose one film director who has made several films based on Shakespeare's plays (Welles, Olivier, Zeffirelli,

Branagh). Compare two or more films by this director in order to identify some characteristics of style, technique, and presentation that exemplify this director's work. What is unique and distinctive about this director's films? How do the films present a particular interpretation of or viewpoint on the plays?

Focus on Reviews. Do some research to locate three or four reviews of a Shakespeare film that were published shortly after the film's release. Read and synthesize the reviews. Did reviewers agree about the qualities of the film? What did contemporary reviewers like and dislike about it? What aspects of the film were controversial? How do those reviews compare to more recent assessments of the film?

Focus on Transformation. Shakespeare plays have often been "loosely" adapted, in both comic and tragic modes. Choose one recent adaptation (*10 Things I Hate About You, O,* or *Scotland, Pa.,* for example) and write a critical analysis of the film as a remake of the Shakespeare play. How does the film transform Shakespeare into a different time and place? How effective is this transformation?

Focus on a Scene. Choose one scene from a play you are interested in, and write a comparative analysis of two or more films' presentation of that scene. Pay attention to detail—look at camera movement and position, acting, and other elements of film technique. Write a detailed close reading of the scene, one which analyzes the key differences in the way each version is presented and the significance of those differences for your understanding of the scene.

Focus on Popular Culture. In addition to the Shakespeare plays themselves, most feature films also make many references to the popular culture of their times. This can happen through the presence of actors that audiences know from other films, the use of visual allusions to other texts or films, product placement, and any number of other cinematic echoes and allusions. (Think of Mel Gibson as Hamlet, for example, or the omnipresence of advertising logos in Luhrmann's *William Shakespeare's Romeo + Juliet.*) Write an analysis of the way a particular film draws upon and uses popular cultural imagery and references to reach an audience. What happens when Shakespeare is reinvented in the context of popular culture?

GLOSSARY

Auteur The French phrase simply means "author." It interprets film as the result of a director's particular point of view rather than seeing it as a more collaborative effort.

Cut An edit that shifts the action to a new camera location.

Deep focus A focusing technique which permits close and distant objects to remain simultaneously in focus.

Dissolve A technique for indicating where one scene ends and another begins by having the image slowly disappear.

Dolly A device by means of which a camera rolls on a track or on a cart around the action as the film runs.

EXT A standard screenplay abbreviation for exterior.

Fade to black A technique for indicating where one scene ends and another begins by having the screen go black before the next image appears.

Film noir The French phrase literally means "dark" or "black" film. It's a style of film in which darkness and the urban environment predominate. The themes are often grim and violent; they are intended to produce a feeling of despair. The style was particularly popular in the late 1940s and early 1950s.

Flashback Those moments when the film is interrupted by earlier action being inserted into the chronology of the narrative. The technique is often used to fill in backstory quickly or to start the film at the beginning of a narrative after a framing device has been employed.

German Expressionism In film studies, the movement in Germany between the wars (1918–1939) in which symbolism and startling mise-en-scene were used as an effective substitute for well-funded film production.

151

INT A standard screenplay abbreviation for interior.

Intercutting A back-and-forth editing movement which allows the audience to compare scenes taking place in different locations or at different times. Also known as **crosscutting**.

Metadrama The various ways in which a work of art comments on its status as art. So, Shakespeare's frequent use of a play-within-the-play ("The Mousetrap" in *Hamlet,* for example) is metadramatic. Films which draw attention to themselves as film are similarly metadramatic.

Mise-en-scene The French phrase literally means "putting into the scene." It includes all of the visual elements that contribute to what viewers see. This term may include setting, costume, makeup, lighting, staging, and acting; it may be limited to only those details and objects which appear in a shot or in the background to create a theme or an atmosphere.

Pan A camera movement where the position of the camera is vertically fixed but swivels horizontally to take in a wide sweep of the action.

Storyboard A series of visual sketches (which look rather like a comic book) that represent each shot or sequence in the film.

Tight shot A shot that pulls the camera in close to the subject and narrows the field of view.

Voice-over A story-telling effect in which we hear an actor speaking off-stage while we watch something else happen. Voice-over often occurs when a narrator is telling a story in flashback or remembering something that has happened earlier.

Wide shot A shot filmed with the camera at a distance using a wide-angle lens. The camera takes in a large background behind the subject in order to achieve a feeling of spaciousness.

REFERENCES

Behrens, Laurence, and Leonard J. Rosen. "Good Take, Sweet Prince: *Hamlet* on Film." *Writing and Reading across the Curriculum*. 8th ed. New York: Longman, 2003. 711–843.

Bordwell, David, and Kristin Thompson. "The Power of *Mise-en-Scene*." *Film Art: An Introduction*. 8th ed. New York: McGraw-Hill, 2006. 157–174.

Cartmell, Deborah. *Interpreting Shakespeare on Screen*. New York: St. Martin's, 2000.

Crowl, Samuel. *Shakespeare and Film. A Norton Guide*. New York: W. W. Norton, 2008.

Ebert, Roger. "10 Things I Hate about You." Rev. *Chicago Sun-Times* Mar. 31, 1999. rogerebert.suntimes.com.

----. "Titus." Rev. *Chicago Sun-Times* Jan. 21, 2000. rogerebert.suntimes.com.

Frye, Northrop. *Anatomy of Criticism: Four Essays*. Princeton: Princeton UP, 1957.

Hindle, Maurice. *Studying Shakespeare on Film*. New York: Palgrave Macmillan, 2007.

Keyishian, Harry. "Shakespeare and the Movie Genre: The Case of *Hamlet*." Russell Jackson, ed. *The Cambridge Companion to Shakespeare on Film*. Cambridge: Cambridge UP, 2000. 72–81.

Manvell, Roger. *Shakespeare and the Film*. New York: Praeger Publishers, 1971.

Morris, Wesley. "'Titus': Shakespeare in War." Rev. *The San Francisco Examiner* Jan. 28, 2000: C2. www.sfgate.com.

Pearce, Craig, and Baz Luhrmann. *William Shakespeare's Romeo + Juliet: The Contemporary Film, The Classic Play*. New York: Bantam Doubleday Dell, 1996.

Sragow, Michael. "Lear Meets the Energy Vampire." Salon.com Sept. 21, 2000. archive.salon.com/ent/col/srag/2000/0921/kurosawa/index.html.

Welsh, James M., Richard Vela, and John C. Tibbetts, ed. *Shakespeare into Film*. New York: Checkmark Books, 2002.